T0122012

death | burial

RESURRECTION

Transformed into His Likeness

CORNELIUS JOHNSON

iUniverse, Inc.
Bloomington

Death, Burial, Resurrection
Transformed into His Likeness

Unless otherwise noted, all Scripture quotations are taken from the Holy Bible, New International Version. NIV. Copyright 1973, 1978, 1984 by International Bible Society. Used by permission of Zondervan. All rights reserved.

Scripture quotations marked Amplified are taken from The Amplified Bible, New Testament. Copyright 1954, 1958, 1987, by the Lockman Foundation. Used by permission.

Scripture quotations marked KJV are taken from the King James Version of the Bible (public domain).

Scripture quotations marked NKJV are taken from The Holy Bible, New King James Version. Copyright 1979, 1980, 1982 by Thomas Nelson, Inc. Used by permission. All rights reserved.

iUniverse books may be ordered through booksellers or by contacting:

iUniverse
1663 Liberty Drive
Bloomington, IN 47403
www.iuniverse.com
1-800-Authors (1-800-288-4677)

Because of the dynamic nature of the Internet, any Web addresses or links contained in this book may have changed since publication and may no longer be valid. The views expressed in this work are solely those of the author and do not necessarily reflect the views of the publisher, and the publisher hereby disclaims any responsibility for them.

ISBN: 978-1-4502-6932-2 (sc)
ISBN: 978-1-4502-6934-6 (dj)
ISBN: 978-1-4502-6933-9 (ebk)

Printed in the United States of America
iUniverse rev. date: 11/11/2010

This book is dedicated to the billions of people on this earth who want to get to know their creator, who find themselves in situations searching for answers and wondering, Does God truly exist and love me?

To the people who are tired of traditional church and seek something they can apply to their daily lives, and to the billions of new and not-yet-believers who are struggling to find the truth.

To the spiritual leaders who made an impact in my life, thank you and may God continue to bless you in all you do.

Finally, to my wife Tiffany who was a vital part in this project, who encouraged me never to give up and to become the man God created me to become before the foundation of this world. I love you!

Contents

Preface

God has placed it in my heart to create a book that will help anyone gain understanding and the ability to apply God's Word to their everyday life, no matter what their Christian education level or denomination may be.

Regardless of what book you read, you should gain some understanding from it. There are numerous books out on the market for us to read about subjects from economics and space flight to basket weaving. They all have one purpose in mind, and that is to give the reader knowledge on a particular subject.

Prior to starting any project you must first set a goal. The goal for this project is to reveal God's love for you and show you how to establish and develop a lasting relationship with him.

If you study Jesus's ministry, you will notice that He spent a lot of time with nonbelievers. This was one of the reasons people didn't want to believe that he was the Messiah. However, to gain people for the kingdom of God, Jesus had to be around all types of people, and he had to speak to them in a way they could understand and relate to.

Today I believe Jesus's ministry is our example for drawing the unsaved into the kingdom of God. Although God's Word must not be changed, I believe we must change the way it is delivered to the people. We cannot afford to miss opportunities to reach these people simply because they can't relate to the message. People need to be able to practically apply the Word of God to their everyday lives.

Before I am able to achieve this goal, I need your active participation. What I need you to do now is say this short prayer to gain understanding as you read this book.

Praying for Understanding

Father God, I ask that you open my heart and my mind so that I can hear you clearly. Allow the eyes of my understanding to be opened so that I can know your ways and how to develop the right relationship with you. Allow me to walk in alignment with you and to fulfill the plans that you have already prepared for my life. Thank you for ordering my steps, for that has brought me here to this special moment. I receive your love, your wisdom, and your knowledge so that I may be able to apply your Word in my daily life. In Jesus's name, amen.

Introduction

Religion. I would like you to throw, everything you know about the subject out the window before you begin reading this book. This book was written to teach you not about religion but about how to develop a lasting relationship with Jesus Christ.

In fact, the less you know about religion, the better, because religion deals with customs and traditions. Customs and traditions are valuable, but building a relationship with Jesus Christ is a matter of the heart.

Webster's dictionary defines *relationship* as "the state of being related or interrelated. The relation connecting or binding participants in a relationship as a kinship. The state of affairs existing between those having relations or dealings. A romantic or passionate attachment."

There is one thing we all have in common and want in our daily lives, and that is to have healthy relationships and someone to love. This is proven with the numerous dating service advertisements on TV, print media, and the Internet.

Have you ever asked yourself why so many people are searching for the perfect relationship? Let me ask you a couple of questions. If you haven't thought about these, please take time right now and reflect for a moment. I want you to be honest when you ask yourself these questions. You may want to take a notepad and write down your thoughts.

Why do we find ourselves always looking for love? Why do we find ourselves searching for that perfect relationship? Why in the midst of a current relationship do you find yourself longing for something else, but you just can't put your finger on what's missing? You don't understand it, but one thing you do know is that you feel incomplete and won't be satisfied until you obtain it.

Let me explain something. God loves you, and he desires an intimate relationship with you. When God created us, he placed something within our spirits that connects us directly to him. This inward part of our being constantly longs for that missing ingredient, which is intimacy with our Creator. Many people attempt to fulfill this void by searching outside themselves, maybe in another person, in a bottle, or in drugs. I'm here to tell you that if you are one of those people, you are looking in the wrong place.

This intimate relationship was first demonstrated in the Garden of Eden between God and Adam. Prior to the fall of mankind, God fellowshipped daily with Adam in the midst of the garden of Eden. But after the fall of mankind, our spirits were separated from God, and we have been searching for that type of relationship ever since.

So God created man in his own image, in the image of God he created him; male and female he created them. (Genesis 1:27)

Not only did God design our physical appearance, but also our total being. This includes the way we think, the way we feel, and the way we exercise our will. No one knows us better than our Creator. This loving relationship that you are longing for has already been established and demonstrated by God.

For God so loved the world that he gave his one and only Son, that whoever believes in him shall not perish but have eternal life. (John 3:16)

The choice is yours. I am here to tell you that if you want to experience a true relationship with someone who loves you more than you love yourself, someone who loves you unconditionally, and someone who will give you complete direction for your life, I encourage you to try God.

Decide today that you will begin to develop your relationship with God. The only way that you can build this relationship is by acknowledging him and spending time with him.

You may think that developing a relationship with God will require a lot of time and special training. That statement is so far from the truth! You may be asking yourself, where do I start? What do I need to do to spend time with God?

The first thing that you need to do is begin reading the Bible. Do not become discouraged if you don't understand a lot of what you're reading. But the secret to this is before you begin to read, pray and ask God for understanding and insight, and you will receive it. As you spend time daily in the Word of God, you will begin to learn his ways, and this is the key to finding out your purpose and ultimate destiny.

The second way to begin building that relationship with God is to talk to him. How can you develop a relationship with someone if you don't talk to them? As a nonbeliever or a new Christian, you may be asking yourself, What can I talk about with God? Is there a certain way that I have to speak to God?

Well, let me clear this up for you. There is no special way to have a conversation with God. There is no certain prayer or ritual, nor do you have to hold a certain position in a church to communicate with God. The only thing you must do is make yourself available to him.

When speaking to God, remember that God is not only your Creator but a loving Father who longs for your companionship. Open your heart to him, be truthful, and don't hold anything back because he already knows what is in your heart.

What I love about God is that no matter what I may be going through in this life or when I fall short, I can always go to him for forgiveness. He loves me so much that he will never leave me or forsake me.

No matter where you find yourself at this present time, regardless of what you have done in the past or any sins you may have committed, nothing can change how God feels toward you. God's love for you is unconditional!

I need you to understand something equally important: the sin factor. God hates sin. Sin cannot dwell in his presence, and if you have sin in your life, it will spiritually separate you from him. However, the good news is that he knows that no one is without sin, and if you ask him for forgiveness, he will forgive you.

***If we claim to be without sin, we deceive ourselves
and the truth is not in us. If we confess our sins, he***

is faithful and just and will forgive us our sins and purify us from all unrighteousness. If we claim we have not sinned, we make him out to be a liar and his word has no place in our lives. (1 John 1:8–10)

As you begin to develop your relationship with God and are following his words, you will begin to see your life transforming into his image. This is God's purpose for all his children.

This book is divided into three sections: Death, Burial, and Resurrection. You may presume that I'll be addressing the death, burial, and resurrection of Jesus Christ. Yes, this is of great importance because what Jesus accomplished for us is our example and now serves as the foundation of our transformation and ultimate divine purpose. As you read through this book, you will see examples of what Jesus accomplished for you, and you will be able to apply it to your life.

I. In the Beginning

Chapter 1
Rewards

Reward is something that you receive for doing something good or useful, something offered or given for services performed, a bonus, lagniappe, or premium.[1]

You maybe wondering, why did I start off talking about rewards? Well, I believe that if you want to gain someone's attention you need to let them know what they will achieve from listening to you. How can this enhance your life? Well, I'm here to let you know there is a reward to be gained on the other side of every *temporary* problem or challenge that you face in life. Yes, I did say *temporary*. No matter what you maybe going through right now, it is only temporary. Do not turn your temporary problem into a permanent one.

Throughout my life I've heard people say, "Why do I always find myself in the same situation?" Many people turn their temporary problem into a permanent one because they have failed to grow and learn what God needed them to learn. Our tests and trials are used to develop us into the men and women God designed us to become. The wisdom and knowledge that we acquire during our tests will be needed to propel us into our next assignments.

As a student in school you are taught on various subject matters. Now after you learn and practice the material, how does a teacher verify that you have obtained the knowledge in a particular subject? A test! During your test, are your teachers allowed to give you the answers? No, of course not. You prove your proficiency by passing the test. So how are you doing on your test?

An example of this is when God allowed Moses to spend numerous years in the desert not because he killed the Egyptian but because God knew he had to lead the children of Israel out of Egypt through the desert on the way to the Promised Land. God knew the children of Israel were going to turn away from him and would spend the next forty years in the desert.

God placed Moses in that situation to gain firsthand experience in order to help the children of Israel. As you can see, many times what you are going through is not always about you. Sometimes God allows situations to occur in your life in order for you to help someone in your future.

I encourage you to learn what God needs you to learn, because if you don't, you may find yourself repeating it again. Don't try to figure out God. Allow him to be God in your life, and do not concern yourself with questions of how.

I have also heard people say, "You don't know the trouble I'm going though!" But God will not allow you to be tested beyond what you can bear. First ***Corinthians 10:13 says, "No temptation has seized you except what is common to man. And***

God is faithful; he will not let you be tempted beyond what you can bear. But when you are tempted, he will also provide a way out so that you can stand up under it."

Now the Word of God tells us that we can withstand in our tests. I repeat, if you don't want to find yourself in the same situation over and over again, you need to pass the test and learn what God needs you to learn. If you are anything like me, you only want to face a difficult situation once, and the key to this is take time out and ask the Father, "What do I need to learn from this situation, and what steps do I need to take in order to win?"

No, in all these things we are more than conquerors through him who loved us. (Romans 8:37)

Now that's good news! The word *conquer* means to gain or acquire by force of arms; to overcome by force of arms; to gain mastery over or win by overcoming obstacles or opposition; to overcome by mental or moral power. God has given us our outcome before we face any situation that occurs in our life. He didn't promise us that we would not have to confront difficult circumstances. However, he did promise us that we were more than conquerors through him who loves us!

I don't know about you, but I love that outcome. Think about it, if you already knew the outcome of a situation before you went through it, wouldn't that make facing the problem that much easier? Next time you have a situation appear in your life, approach it with your heart and mind set knowing that "I will prevail!"

Faith Is the Key

By faith Enoch was taken from this life, so that he didn't experience death; he could not be found, because God had taken him away. For before he was taken, he was commended as one who pleased God. And without faith it is impossible to please God, because anyone who comes to him must believe that he exists and that he rewards those who earnestly seek him. (Hebrews 11:5–6)

In order to become "more than a conqueror" in the trials you face in life, you must exercise your faith. The problem with many Christians is that they don't exercise their faith in all things—or you may be thinking, "I don't believe in that faith stuff." Actually you utilize faith every day without even realizing it. You make your plans for tomorrow, you walk out every day and get into your car, expecting it to start and safely take you to your destination, and carry out many other day-to-day activities besides these.

You must utilize your faith in every area of your life even those "small" situations that normally don't overly concern you. Many people don't use faith until a "huge" problem occurs, and then when they don't get the results they expected to achieve, they blame God and all the while don't understand why it didn't come to pass. You can't conquer a giant until you have successful conquered a grasshopper. Our faith is like a muscle, and the more you exercise it, the stronger it becomes, so that when the next challenge arises you are prepared to win.

Earlier I mentioned that with every problem you go through, there is a reward on the other side. I once heard a minister say, "The bigger the problem, the bigger the reward." I agree with that statement, and we will examine the lives of two men in particular in the Scriptures that will prove that statement. I encourage you to take out your Bible and go back and review the passages for yourself.

Abraham's Assignment

Let's turn to the book of Genesis and take a look at an example of faith exercised in the life of Abraham. In Genesis 12:1, God addresses Abraham: "Leave your country, your people and your father's household and go to the land I will show you." In that verse the Lord was telling Abraham what he wanted him to do. In the immediately following verses God told Abraham his reward, the purpose that would be fulfilled:

> *I will make you into a great nation*
> *   and I will bless you;*
> *I will make your name great*
> *   and you will be a blessing.*
> *I will bless those who bless you*
> *   and whoever curses you I will curse;*
> *and all peoples on the earth*
> *   will be blessed through you.*
> *(Genesis 12:2–3)*

I believe the Lord told Abraham the reward prior to his departure because he knew if Abram didn't have anything to focus on, it would have been easier for him to give up. Does this sound familiar? I admit when I first started my walk with God, I had a habit of giving up right in the middle of challenging situations. Now that I have matured in my relationship with God, I take time out and ask him to show me the reward and the purpose that is located on the other side of this problem. This is what motivates me to overcome the situation. I encourage you to do the same, and I pray that you stand firm and push through your situation because God will not fail you!

Once Abraham departed his country and his father's household with his wife Sarah and his nephew Lot, this action proved his obedience and faith in what God promised. During the journey, Abram continued to spend time developing his relationship with the Lord, and God gave him further instructions and continued ordering his steps toward the Negev.

The Situation

Genesis 12:10 states "Now there was a famine in the land, and Abram [his name before God called him Abraham] went down to Egypt to live there for a while because the famine was severe." So we see here that Abraham received his assignment and began his journey with Sarah, his nephew Lot, and their entire household. Obviously, Sarah and Lot had to trust Abraham's decision, or else they might have begun to criticize him, thinking he had lost his mind to have them in the middle of a country in famine.

This type of worry and frustration would be expected from someone who did not have a relationship with the Lord—or perhaps more naturally from someone who did not receive the assignment. You see, the Lord came to Abraham and gave him the instruction. The Lord didn't go to Sarah or Lot, so they may not have totally understood what was going on during that testing period.

When you completely put your trust in someone in authority, you will not challenge them but will obey them without objection. And when you put your trust in God, you should obey him freely because you love him and you trust that he knows what is best for your life.

Pause & Reflect

Has there ever been a time in your life when you shared an idea or a dream with someone, and they responded with negativity, or have you made a negative comment against someone else's vision or dream?

When Abraham departed his father's land, his wife Sarah could have said something negative, but she didn't. She may not have heard what God told Abram, but she knew what type of relationship he had established with God.

When God gives an assignment, it is something far beyond our natural ability and will require faith. As we saw earlier pointed out in **Hebrews 11:6, without faith it is impossible to please God.** Your faith is revealed when you take action on God's Word. The action may seem foolish to all those around you, but know that God is ordering your steps. Move out in faith, and he will walk with you.

Doubt and Unbelief

During your walk and development with your Father, there may be times when doubt, unbelief, or disobedience will seep in and cause you to fall short. However, God is still able to deliver you in the midst of your failures. He is not a Father who is there only when you do the right thing. He loves you unconditionally, and he will never leave you or forsake you.

> *Now along Abraham's journey, he encountered a situation in which he allowed doubt to enter in. This occurred when he was on his way to Egypt: he told his wife Sarah to lie. He told her, "I know what a beautiful woman you are. When the Egyptians see you, they will say, 'This is his wife.' Then they will kill me but will let you live. Say you are my sister, so that I will be treated well for your sake and my life will be spared because of you" (Genesis 12:11–13).*

The book of Romans records Abram as the father of the faithful because he believed God (4:11–12, 16). However, during this encounter with the Egyptians he responded with fear, believing that the Egyptians would kill him because of his beautiful wife. There may be times in your life when you stumble and fall. Experiencing doubt and unbelief is natural as you are developing your relationship with God.

However, he expects us to mature as we continue in our Christian walk, just as you expect your children to mature as they grow older. As you begin to meditate on the Word of God and place your trust in him, doubt and unbelief will begin to vanish.

But this must be a daily practice in your life. As you begin to read your Bible, you will begin to learn his ways. Your faith will start to grow, and you will begin to trust him.

Romans 10:17 states, "Faith comes from hearing the message, and the message is heard through the word of Christ." I encourage you not to allow doubt or unbelief to hinder your growth and steal the promises of God from your heart. When you feel doubt, I want you to stop and begin meditating on the Word of God. Tell him what is on your mind and that you are starting to have doubt but you want to believe. Ask the Father to strengthen you in this area of weakness so that you will push past your doubt and achieve what God ordained for you to accomplish.

Grace and Mercy

Now, once Abraham and his family arrived in Egypt, the Egyptians did just as he had predicted. They saw that Sarah was a very beautiful woman, and when the pharaoh's officials saw her, they praised her to Pharaoh, and she was taken into his palace. Pharaoh treated Abraham well for her sake, and he acquired sheep and cattle, male and female donkeys, male and female servants, and camels.

You may be thinking, since Abraham was disobedient in Egypt when he lied, representing Sarah as his wife, that God would have allowed him to lose his wife to Pharaoh. However, our Father is a God of love, and even in our unfaithfulness, God is always faithful to his promise. In the midst of our failures, God will always provide an open door, but you must have the faith and courage to walk through it.

How many times have you done wrong and nothing happened to you? How many times have you received punishment for something you did wrong, but the penalty you received was less than you deserved? You may think you got off easily, or maybe you didn't even get caught. But none of your actions are hidden from God, and this just demonstrates God's grace and mercy in action.

Let me explain something to you. Your actions will cause reactions. If you break the law and get caught, you are going to receive punishment for your action. That's a fact, and there is nothing you or I can do about that. However, many times God's grace and mercy are demonstrated, and he can control the outcome.

Let me add clarity to this. I'm not saying that if you commit a crime, get caught, stand before a judge, and then repent and ask

God to forgive you, you won't go to jail. No, I'm not saying that at all. If you commit a crime and are convicted, you will serve the punishment decreed by the court because your action caused that reaction. So don't go around blaming God because you got caught up in this bad position.

I want you to be aware that God's grace and mercy operate even when you are undeserving, but you should not go through life abusing this fact: but rather grow, mature, and become what God ordained you to become.

The Open Door

The Lord inflicted serious diseases on Pharaoh and his household because of Abram's wife Sarai [her name before she was renamed Sarah]. So Pharaoh summoned Abram. "What have you done to me?" he said. "Why didn't you tell me she was your wife? Why did you say, 'She is my sister,' so that I took her to be my wife? Now then, here is your wife. Take her and go!" Then Pharaoh gave orders about Abram to his men, and they sent him on his way, with his wife and everything he had. (Genesis 12:17–20)

Remember, no matter what situation you are going through right now as you read this book, God has already established an open door. You may be wondering, "What is an open door? How do I find this open door?" Simply put, an open door is an opportunity, and you find this open door by asking the Father to reveal it to you so that you will be able to walk through it.

You may be thinking that is easier said than done. To walk through an open door requires faith. As I mentioned earlier, you must start exercising your faith muscle now so that when it's time to face your giants, you will overcome them all.

Pause & Reflect

If your life is in total chaos because of your own disobedience, you now have the chance to make it right. Ask the Father to forgive you and to provide you with another opportunity, an open door. Commit your life to daily fellowship with the Father, by talking with him and studying his Word. He will then place an idea in your spirit or may send someone in this moment to help you.

Don't fall back into your old mind-set and lack of faith, thinking this will not work. It is vitally important for you to use your faith in all things, even "small" things. This door of opportunity is God-ordained for you. Now it is up to you to take action and walk thought it. Start conquering those grasshoppers so when the giants come into your life, you will look back over your experience with God (his track record) and with confidence walk through that open door.

David's Assignment

Now we are going to take a look at the life of David, the son of Jesse. After the Lord rejected Saul as king of Israel after he turned away from following God's instruction, the Lord sent the prophet Samuel to anoint the next king of Israel. Samuel was sent to the house of Jesse in Bethlehem because the Lord had chosen one of his sons to be king. (Keep in mind that Jesse had a total of eight sons.)

When they arrived, Samuel saw Eliab and thought, "Surely the Lord's anointed stand here before the Lord."

But the LORD said to Samuel. "Do not consider his appearance or his height, for I have rejected him. The LORD does not look at the things man looks at. Man looks at the outward appearance but the LORD looks at the heart." (1 Samuel 16:6–8)

No matter where you are in your life today, no matter how low or high you may feel right now, what matters most to God is what is in your heart. Don't get discouraged if someone looks down on you because of your current position, because if your heart is right towards God, he is going to raise you up, right in the presence of your enemies.

Jesse brought each of his sons to Samuel to be anointed as the next king of Israel except his youngest son who was out in the fields taking care of the sheep. Samuel asked Jesse whether these were all his sons. Jesse replied "There is still the youngest who is attending the sheep."

When David arrived he was described as ruddy, with fine appearance, and handsome features, and the Lord instructed

Samuel to anoint him because he was the one. You would think that after David was anointed by Samuel to be the next king of Israel, he would have refused to go back out to the fields caring for the sheep. But David continued serving in the field, while all along God was developing great leadership skills within him that he would later need in his calling.

During that time Israel was at war with the Philistines. The Philistines had a champion named Goliath. He was over nine feet tall. No one in Israel would face him, and all were terrified due to Goliath's size and appearance. Goliath was so confident in his strength that he said, *"Choose a man and have him come down to me. If he is able to fight and kill me, we will become your subjects" (1 Samuel 17:8–9).* Keep in mind that Goliath was there with his entire army, but the challenge he issued was for a man to defeat him, not his army.

Now, David went to visit his brothers at the encampment against the Philistines, because his father instructed him to go see about them and bring them food, and when he arrived at the camp with his brothers, Goliath came out in the open on the battle field, repeating the same thing.

David's Reward

When David heard Goliath's taunt, he asked what the King would give to the person who killed the giant.

The king will give great wealth to the man who kills him. He will also give him his daughter in marriage and will exempt his father's family from taxes in Israel. (1 Samuel 17:25)

Now once Eliab, David's oldest brother, heard him speak he asked David, *"Why have you come down here? And with whom did you leave those few sheep in the desert? I know how conceited you are and how wicked your heart is; you came down only to watch the battle"* (verse 28).

Now why do you think Eliab made such harsh accusations against his brother David? I believe jealously rose up in Eliab's heart toward his brother, and he didn't understand David's relationship with God. David's relationship with God produced a confidence that looked like arrogance to those around him. However, David was in no way conceited in himself, but had great faith in his God.

David's Situation

When Saul saw David, he replied, ***"You are not able to go out against this Philistine and fight him; you are only a boy, and he has been a fighting man from his youth" (1 Samuel 17:33).***

You see, Saul was looking at David's outward appearance, not realizing the faith and trust David had developed in God on the inside. Think back over your life when you wanted to accomplish something and shared the desire with someone, and they told you that you couldn't do it. They told you that because it looked like an impossibility, but remember with God all things are possible.

David began to tell Saul his previous experiences (his track record) and said:

> ***Your servant has been keeping his father's sheep. When a lion or a bear came and carried off a sheep from the flock, I went after it, struck it and rescued the sheep from its mouth. When it turned on me, I seized it by its hair, struck it and killed it. Your servant has killed both the lion and the bear; this uncircumcised Philistine will be like one of them, because he has defied the armies of the living God. (verses 34–36)***

So David triumphed over the Philistine with a sling and a stone; without a sword in his hand he struck down the Philistine and killed him.

> ***David ran and stood over him. He took hold of the Philistine's sword and drew it from the scabbard.***

After he killed him, he cut off his head with the sword. (verses 50–51)

In today's military, men and women go through numerous types of boot camp training. During their training period, they are put in difficult challenges, not to fail but to learn how carry on in these situations. Once they are competent in the situations that occurr in that training environment, they will not panic and give up in real combat.

You may be in a "boot camp" challenge in your own personal life right now. But remember it is a training period. You are being taught how to handle different types of situations because what God has in store for your future will require you to draw on the experiences you are now undergoing.

Pause & Reflect

Have people ever looked down on you because of the way you looked, your background, or the situation you are currently in? Do you feel that you are not at the level or place in your life where God can use you? God doesn't look at your outward appearance. He looks at what is most important, and that is your heart.

That's the difference between God and man. Man looks only at the outward appearance. People tend to judge you before they truly get to know you. Have you ever heard that statement, "Never judge a book by its cover"? When you read the story of David's life, you can get a glimpse of how God thinks.

I encourage you not to give up. It's not always about you. God is allowing you to go through these situations so that you can help someone else. Continue to stand firm, push through, and become the person God ordained you to become. Continue to fight the good fight of faith! Greater is he that is in you than he that is in the world (see 1 John 4:4).

Your Assignment

I believe that one of the most asked questions in our lives is, What is my purpose here on this earth? This important question was addressed by Rick Warren, author of *The Purpose-Driven Life* and senior pastor of Saddleback Church in California.

I am not able to tell you your individual purpose. However, I can tell you that you were created for the glory of God, and your purpose on this earth is vital for his kingdom. Since your birth, God placed you on a path to gain all the necessary knowledge to accomplish the purpose you were created for. Only *you* can fulfill the purpose you were designed to fulfill. That's how uniquely God created *you*. You are so important to the kingdom of God. That is one of the main reasons the enemy tries to sidetrack you and tempts you to give up: he knows you are the only one to carry out the vision for your life. As you develop your personal relationship with the Father, began to inquire about your future. He desires to tell you your purpose and give you divine instructions for your life. Now, once he reveals your purpose, he will begin to process you, place you on your route, and position you to excel in life.

REVIEW

- There is a reward to be gained on the other side of every *temporary* problem or challenge that you face in life.

- Without faith it is impossible to please God. Begin to utilize faith in every aspect of your life.

- Do not allow doubt and unbelief to hinder your growth and steal the promises of God from your heart.

- Whatever you are going through right now, look at it as if you are in training, like boot camp. God is teaching you, and what he has in store for you will require you to draw on your past experiences.

- You were created for the glory of God, and your purpose on this earth is vital for his kingdom. Since your birth, God placed you on a path to gain all the necessary knowledge to accomplish the purpose you were created for.

PRAYER

Father, before I was placed in my mother's womb, you gave me a purpose to fulfill on this earth. You placed inside me everything that I would ever need to accomplish my mission. I ask you to reveal your purpose for my life. Order my steps, and give me the strength and courage to go through every obstacle I encounter, because I know you are training and equipping me with the necessary skills to complete my task. I now know that it's not always about me, but to further the kingdom of God. I know that I am unique, and only I can accomplish what you ordained me to accomplish. I accept my destiny, and I thank you now for all you've done and already prepared for me. In Jesus's name, amen.

II. The Death

Chapter 2

How Much God the Father Loves You

For God so loved the world that he gave his one and only Son, that whoever believes in him shall not perish but have eternal life. For God did not send his Son into the world to condemn the world, but to save the world through him. (John 3:16–17)

From the beginning of time God has always loved you. He has given you a plan for your life and with that plan the ability to have dominion on this earth. He created you in his own image and loved you over all of his creations.

Although Eve was deceived by the devil, and she and Adam disobeyed the Father by eating from the tree of knowledge of good and evil, God still loved us. John 3:16–17 reveals that love and the plan that would allow us to again commune and develop the true relationship that he desires with everyone.

You may be asking yourself, How can I believe that God loves me, because I'm always finding myself in situations that I feel separate me from him?—or If God truly loves me, why does it feel like he doesn't? The fact that God loves you must be established in your heart, and it will take faith in the Word of God for you to believe this. The trials and temptations of life will come, but in spite of these things, you must know this important truth.

I received an e-mail from a friend, and I believe it clearly illustrates the purpose of these trials. The e-mail told a story about a women's Bible study group, and I would like to share this story with you.

There was group of women in a Bible study on the book of Malachi. As they were studying chapter 3, they came across a verse that says, "He will sit as a refiner and purifier of silver." This verse puzzled the women, and they wondered what this statement meant about the character and nature of God.

One of them offered to find out about the process of refining silver and get back to the group at their next Bible study. That week she called up a silversmith and made an appointment to watch him at work. She didn't mention anything about the reason for her interest in silver beyond her curiosity about the process of refining silver.

As she watched the silversmith, he held a piece of silver over the fire and let it heat up. He explained that, in refining silver, one needed to hold the silver in the middle of the fire where the flames were hottest so as to burn away all the impurities.

The woman thought about God holding us in such a hot spot—then she thought again about the verse, that He sits as a refiner and purifier of silver. She asked the silversmith if it was true that he had to sit there in front of the fire the whole time the silver was being refined.

The man answered yes, he not only had to sit there holding the silver, but he had to keep his eyes on the silver the entire time it was in the fire. For if the silver was left even a moment too long in the flames, it would be destroyed.

The woman was silent for a moment. Then she asked the silversmith, "How do you know when the silver is fully refined?" He smiled at her and answered, "Oh, that's the easy part: when I see my image reflected in it." If today you are feeling the heat of the fire, remember that God has his eye on you and will keep his hand on you and watch over you until he sees his image in you. (The author of this story is unknown.)

This story is a perfect example of how our heavenly Father is continuously molding us into the people he created us to be.

Yet, O LORD, you are our Father.
We are the clay, you are the potter;
we are all the work of your hand. (Isaiah 64:8)

God is actively at work in our lives even when we think he is not aware of our problems. His Spirit is constantly speaking and guiding us. However, we can easily miss his voice when we allow the problems of life to overwhelm and burden us.

We all have a past, either good or bad, but our past can play a very important part in who we are today. In the beginning of this book, I told you that God wanted me to be transparent as I wrote, and I will share my experiences with you and how I personally came to the knowledge of God's love operating in my life.

As a child growing up in the inner city, I was exposed to all types of people and their lifestyles. I used to find myself feeling all alone and as if no one truly cared about me. I use to compare my life with other people, wishing that my life could be like theirs. I thought I would be happier if I traded lives with someone else.

In my early teens I began to ask God to help me make it through these times when I felt my life was of no value.

I didn't realize that God was always with me even when I thought I was alone. When I look back over my life and all the situations I was exposed to, I shouldn't be here today or even be the type of person I am now. When I was called into ministry, "my past" hindered me from accepting what God called me to do. I thought I had to have the "perfect" life in order to fulfill the call to ministry.

One day as I was spending time with God, I began to tell him all the reasons why I shouldn't be called to spread his love. I begin to explain that I didn't want any part in shaping other people's lives and above all didn't want the additional responsibility. I thought all along that it was hard enough to keep my own life straight! As he began to speak to me, this was the turning point in my life when I finally realized how God had been guiding me throughout my life.

The Holy Spirit asked me a series of questions: "Do you love me?" I replied, *With all of my heart.* "Do you trust me?" I replied, *Unconditionally.* "Do you love helping people?" I replied, *Yes, Lord I do, and I get great joy seeing people happy.*

The Holy Spirit said, "Son, you have a heart of God because God is love. I've placed this gift inside of you from the day you were born. Just look back over your life. Do you remember the situations you were in when I rescued you? You had a very challenging childhood, and you could have turned out another way, but look at you. I guided your footsteps, and you didn't even know it. Those situations you were going through when you didn't know the reason why? I was molding you for what I had planned for you.

"Don't worry about failing! If you lift me up, I'll do the drawing! You just tell them what I instruct you to say, and I'll do the rest. They must make a choice to come to me; you are only responsible for giving them the information. Don't worry my son, I'm always with you."

Perfected Love

God sent his Son Jesus to die for you and me when we didn't even acknowledge him. He sent his Son to die for us when we turned our backs on him. God's love for us is unconditional: no matter how much we sin and fall short of the glory of God, he is faithful to forgive and wash those things away as though they never existed. *"If we confess our sins, he is faithful and just and will forgive us our sins and purify us from all unrighteousness"* *(1 John 1:9).*

> *If you love those who love you, what reward will you get? Are not even the tax collectors doing that? (Matthew 5:46)*

Webster defines love as "(1) strong affection for another arising out of kinship or personal ties. Unselfish loyal and benevolent concern for the good of another.[1]

What I love about God is that he always sets the example. He requires his children to love everyone, and he demonstrated that when he sent his Son Jesus to die on the cross for you and me. How can you not love him!

Pause & Reflect

I would like you to reflect a moment with a couple of questions:

- If you are a parent, are you willing to do whatever it takes to protect your child from an injustice? Would you be willing to allow your child to face a sentence for a stranger?

- If you are not a parent, are you willing to allow someone you truly love to die or face a sentence for a stranger?

As a father, I would lay my life down for my family. However, I would be lying if I told you I would allow them or myself to die for someone who didn't know us or cared nothing about us. Yet God showed his love for all of mankind when we were sinners.

One thing we must remember: God would never ask us to do something he is not willing to do himself. God demonstrated this act when he sent Jesus to die for you and me!

REVIEW

- God's Love for you is unconditional.

- God is actively at work in your life now, and he is molding you into the person he created you to be.

- God's love must be established in your heart even in the midst of tests and trials. It takes faith to believe this kind of love.

Chapter 3
There Can Only Be One

Do not let your hearts be troubled. Trust in God; trust also in me. In my Father's house are many rooms; if it were not so, I would have told you. I am going there to prepare a place for you. And if I go and prepare a place for you, I will come back and take you to be with me that you also may be where I am. You know the way to the place where I am going.

> *Thomas said to him, "Lord, we don't know where you are going, so how can we know the way?"*
>
> *Jesus answered, "I am the way and the truth and the life. No one comes to the Father except through me. If you really knew me, you would know my Father as well. From now on, you do know him and have seen him." (John 14:1–7)*

I've had the opportunity to travel all around the world and meet people of different religions, backgrounds, and customs. One thing many of them held in common was their "belief in God."

Jesus reveals to us that he is the only way to God the Father. He is the one who brought us back into direct relationship with the Father. Some people may argue that this way is too narrow. In reality, it is wide enough for the whole world, if the world chooses to accept it. Instead of worrying about how limited it sounds to have only one way, we should be saying, "Thank God for providing a sure way to get to you!"

Jesus is the visible, tangible image of the invisible God. He is the complete revelation of who God is. Jesus explained to Philip, who wanted to see the Father, that to know him is to know God. The search for God, for truth and reality, begins and ends in Christ Jesus.

He has rescued us from the dominion of darkness and brought us into the kingdom of the Son he loves, in whom we have redemption, the forgiveness of sins.

He is the image of the invisible God, the firstborn over all creation. For by him all things were created: things in heaven and on earth, visible and invisible, whether thrones or powers or rulers or authorities; all things were created by him and for him. He is before all things, and in him all things hold together. And he is the head of the body, the church; he is the beginning and the firstborn from among the dead, so that in everything he might have the supremacy.

For God was pleased to have all his fullness dwell in him, and through him to reconcile to himself all things,

whether things on earth or things in heaven, by making peace through his blood, shed on the cross. (Colossians 1:13–20, NIV APP)

Christ's death provided a way for all people to come to God. It cleared away the sin that kept us from having an effective relationship with God the Father. This doesn't mean that everyone has been automatically saved through his death on the cross. Jesus's death on the cross cleared the way back to the Father for anyone who will *trust* in him. You must believe and accept Jesus to receive your salvation and forgiveness of sins.

Therefore God exalted him to the highest place and gave him the name that is above every name, that at the name of Jesus every knee should bow, in heaven and on earth and under the earth, and every tongue confess that Jesus Christ is Lord, to the glory of God the Father. (Philippians 2:9–11)

Then the eleven disciples went to Galilee, to the mountain where Jesus had told them to go. When they saw him, they worshiped him; but some doubted. Then Jesus came to them and said, "All authority in heaven and on earth has been given to me." (Matthew 28:16–18, NIV APP)

Jesus' life and death on the cross redeemed us from the second death and gave us access to the gift of eternal life. We all have to die one day, and there's nothing you or I can do about it. However, we don't have to experience the second death.

The gift of eternal life isn't automatic through the death of Jesus Christ. You must accept Jesus as your Lord and Savior and repent which will place your name in the Book of Life.

> *Then I saw a great white throne and him who was seated on it. Earth and sky fled from his presence, and there was no place for them. And I saw the dead, great and small, standing before the throne, and books were opened. Another book was opened, which is the book of life. The dead were judged according to what they had done as recorded in the books. The sea gave up the dead that were in it, and death and Hades gave up the dead that were in them, and each person was judged according to what he had done. Then death and Hades were thrown into the lake of fire. The lake of fire is the second death. If anyone's name was not found written in the book of life, he was thrown into the lake of fire. (Revelation 20:11–15)*

If God did not spare angels when they sinned, but sent them to hell, putting them into gloomy dungeons to be held for judgment; if he did not spare the ancient world when he brought the flood on its ungodly people, but protected Noah, a preacher of righteousness, and seven others; if he condemned the cities of Sodom and Gomorrah by burning them to ashes, and made them an example of what is going to happen to the ungodly; and if he rescued Lot, a righteous man, who was distressed by the filthy lives of lawless men (for that righteous man, living among them day after day, was tormented in his righteous soul by the lawless deeds he saw and heard)—if this is so, then the

Lord knows how to rescue godly men from trials and to hold the unrighteous for the day of judgment, while continuing their punishment. (2 Peter 2:4–9)

First, let me say that I'm not discussing the second death to scare you into accepting Christ. As a child I was brought up listening to preachers and my parents telling me about hell—that if I didn't get my life right, I would find myself in hell. I believe they thought that this method would scare me into doing right. I'm here to tell you that it didn't scare me into living right, and I know it won't scare you into living right.

The reason I'm telling you about the second death is because it's a fact, and I want to make sure that you know the consequences of your name not being in the Book of Life. Scaring a person will only make them act correctly for a short period of time, and it won't last because they changed for the wrong reason.

I promised God that I would tell his people what he wants them to know, and I would not compromise my promise to him to make people feel good. I am not responsible for making people accept him and his Son, Jesus. I am only responsible for giving them the information, and it is up to them to choose. I must obey my promise and give you the correct information—and it is up to you to believe.

There was a rich man who was dressed in purple and fine linen and lived in luxury every day. At his gate was laid a beggar named Lazarus, covered with sores and longing to eat what fell from the rich man's table. Even the dogs came and licked his sores.

The time came when the beggar died and the angels carried him to Abraham's side. The rich man also died and was buried. In hell, where he was in torment, he looked up and saw Abraham far away, with Lazarus by his side. So he called to him, "Father Abraham, have pity on me and send Lazarus to dip the tip of his finger in water and cool my tongue, because I am in agony in this fire."

But Abraham replied, "Son remember that in your lifetime you received your good things, while Lazarus received bad things, but now he is comforted here and you are in agony. And besides all this, between us and you a great chasm has been fixed, so that those who want to go from here to you cannot, nor can anyone cross over from there to us."

He answered, "Then I beg you, father, send Lazarus to my father's house, for I have five brothers. Let him warn them, so that they will not also come to this place of torment."

Abraham replied, "They have Moses and the Prophets; let them listen to them."

"No, father Abraham," he said, "but if someone from the dead goes to them, they will repent."

He said to him, "If they do not listen to Moses and the Prophets, they will not be convinced even if someone rises from the dead." (Luke 16:19–31)

In these verses Moses was explaining to the rich man when he was among the living he lived what we would call a very good life. However while the rich man was alive, he felt that he didn't need God, nor did he show God's love. This was shown in his actions by allowing Lazarus to sit by his gate, needing food and maybe even shelter, but the rich man did nothing. You may be wondering, What sin did the rich man commit to end up in hell? Well, I'm not God, and I don't know how God will judge each and every one of us. However, what came to mind when I read those verses was the following passage:

Hearing that Jesus had silenced the Sadducees, the Pharisees got together. One of them, an expert in the law, tested him with this question: "Teacher, which is the greatest commandment in the Law?"

Jesus replied: "'Love the Lord your God with all your heart and with all your soul and with all your mind.' This is the first and greatest commandment. And the second is like it: 'Love your neighbor as yourself.' All the Law and the Prophets hang on these two commandments." (Matthew 22:34–40)

The problem with many of us is that we always try to complicate things. That is what we do with religion. We gain a little bit of knowledge, and then we tend to overanalyze situations. Jesus understood that and made it very simple, explaining to the Pharisees if they just obeyed those two verses they would live the life God desired from them.

I'm hear to tell you the same thing: don't worry about the ten commandments. Just take the two verses Jesus told the Pharisees and apply them to your daily lives, and I promise that you will live the life God desires from you.

You may say, "How can you make a statement like that?" Well, think about it! If you obey those two commandments, you will automatically obey the rest. If you love your neighbor as yourself, you won't lie to them, you won't kill them, and you won't commit adultery or any of the other offenses listed in the Law.

> *Now a man came up to Jesus and asked, "Teacher, what good thing must I do to get eternal life?" … Jesus replied "'Do not murder, do not commit adultery, do not steal, do not give false testimony, honor your father and mother, and love your neighbor as yourself.'"*
>
> *"All these I have kept," the young man said. "What do I still lack?" Jesus answered, "If you want to be perfect, go, sell your possessions and give to the poor, and you will have treasure in heaven. Then come, follow me."*
>
> *When the young man heard this, he went away sad, because he had great wealth.*
>
> *Then Jesus said to his disciples, "I tell you the truth, it is hard for a rich man to enter the kingdom of heaven. Again I tell you, it is easier for a camel to go through the eye of a needle than for a rich man to enter the kingdom of God." (Matthew 19:16–24)*

Let's take a little time to explore what Jesus was telling the young rich man. Jesus was not saying to the rich man that the only way you can gain eternal life is to be poor. That is very far from the truth! Jesus was telling him that he must be willing to give up what he has obtained to gain even more.

God desires his children to depend on him completely. He doesn't want you to place anything above him because, if you do, you have just made that item in your life a "god." Those with wealth tend to believe that they don't need God because they can basically buy anything they need in this life. So with that type of attitude, can they truly depend on God for everything?

Please understand that I am not saying that it is impossible for a rich person to accept Jesus as their Lord and Savior and develop a relationship with God our Father. What I'm saying is that when you have unlimited resources, you may start to believe that you are responsible for your success. You may start to believe that God had nothing to do with your success. What those who are rich need to understand is that God is the one who has given them their gifts and talents. It is God who has ordered their steps, and through God's grace they have accomplished something great.

If that young rich man had given away all his wealth to the poor, don't you think God would have honored that and given him back all he had given away plus much more? God honors our faithfulness, and there will be times that you may feel that you are going backward instead of forward. Just keep your faith in Jesus Christ. There may be times when you have to take two steps backward today, but that doesn't mean that God won't allow you to take eight steps forward tomorrow.

I beg you, don't be like the two rich men described in these two stories. Trust in our Lord Jesus, repent from your sin, have your name added to the Book of Life, and bypass the second death. God loves you so much, so much that he will not force you to do anything you don't want to do. It is all up to you; the choice is yours.

Pause & Reflect

I'm going to ask you two very important questions, and I need you to think carefully before you respond. I've shown you what is written in the Bible about the second death, and I've backed up my conclusions with supporting scriptures. What I need to know from you is this: "Do you have any proof that hell or the lake of fire does not exist?" The other question: "Are you willing to bet your right to eternal life on your response?"

I truly pray that you don't imitate the rich man in Luke 16:19–31, but it is all up to you. God loves you unconditionally, but he will not force you to love him and accept his Son, Jesus, as your Lord and Savior. You should serve God because you love him and should accept Jesus Christ as your Lord and Savior because you believe what God has told you in his Word. Time is short, and you must choose. Pause right now, search your heart, and make a wise decision.

Jesus: Man or Son of God?

Before we go any further discussing your relationship with God, we need to establish who Jesus Christ is and the price that he paid for us to be back in direct fellowship with God the Father. Many of you may have heard people from other religious backgrounds acknowledge Jesus as a prophet or teacher or by some other title but deny him as the Son of God.

In the book of Luke, Jesus's birth was foretold by the following:

In the sixth month, God sent the angel Gabriel to Nazareth, a town in Galilee, to a virgin pledged to be married to a man named Joseph, a descendant of David. The virgin's name was Mary. The angel went to her and said, "Greetings, you who are highly favored! The Lord is with you ... You will be with child and give birth to a son, and you are to give him the name Jesus. He will be great and will be called the Son of the Most High. The Lord God will give him the throne of his father David, and he will reign over the house of Jacob forever; his kingdom will never end."

"How will this be," Mary asked the angel, "since I am a virgin?"

The angel answered, "The Holy Spirit will come upon you, and the power of the Most High will overshadow you. So the holy one to be born will be called the Son of God." (Luke 1:26–28, 31–35)

Now, through those verses in Luke we have established that an angel of God spoke to Mary, a virgin, and told her she would be overshadowed by the Holy Spirit and become pregnant with Jesus, the Son of God. Naturally speaking, this is impossible, but with God all things are possible. Mary also brought up this fact to the angel who appeared to her by saying, "How will this be, since I am a virgin?" Now please keep in mind during this period of time Mary was engaged to marry Joseph.

This is how the birth of Jesus Christ came about: His mother Mary was pledged to be married to Joseph, but before they came together, she was found to be with child through the Holy Spirit. Because Joseph her husband was a righteous man and did not want to expose her to public disgrace, he had in mind to divorce her quietly.

> *But after he had considered this, an angel of the Lord appeared to him in a dream and said, "Joseph son of David, do not be afraid to take Mary home as your wife, because what is conceived in her is from the Holy Spirit. She will give birth to a son, and you are to give him the name Jesus, because he will save his people from their sins."*
>
> *All this took place to fulfill what the Lord had said through the prophet: "The virgin will be with child and will give birth to a son, and they will call him Immanuel"—which means, "God with us." ...*
>
> *When Joseph woke up, he did what the angel of the Lord had commanded him and took Mary home as his wife. But he had no union with her until she gave birth to a son. And he gave him the name Jesus. (Matthew 1:18–21, 24–25)*

The Book of Matthew states that after Joseph found out that his wife was pregnant with a child prior to their consummating the marriage, he decided that he would divorce Mary quietly. His initial reaction and thinking would have been justified, considering the situation. However Joseph was a just man, and his relationship and faith in God allowed him to believe the dream as a realistic explanation on how Mary became pregnant.

Pause & Reflect

The United States of America is the land of the free and home of the brave. I am proud to be an American citizen, and one thing I love about my country is the freedom to worship freely, no matter what your religious preference. In the past two years I've listened to numerous people giving their different opinions about the divinity of Jesus Christ. I've heard people say that Jesus is not the only way to God. I've also heard numerous people say they believe in God but not in Jesus as Savior.

I want you to understand that Jesus Christ is the only way to God, and when I say God, I mean the God of Abraham, Isaac, and Jacob. I want you also to understand that I'm only telling you what is written in the Bible. "I [Jesus] am the way and the truth and the life. No one comes to the Father except through me" (John 14:6). In this Christian walk we don't choose to believe only certain portions of the Bible. We must believe and learn from the entire Bible. In this Christian walk it comes down to this one fact: Either you believe, or you don't! There is no room for compromise!

Faith is needed to complete this Christian walk. Faith is a firm belief in something for which there is no proof. You may say, "I don't understand the faith principles; I've tried it, but it didn't work." As I pointed out in the beginning of this book, you must start by exercising faith in the little things. Faith is like a muscle: the more you use it, the larger and stronger it becomes.

Without faith it is impossible to please God, because anyone who comes to him must believe that he exists and that he rewards those who earnestly seek him. (Hebrews 11:6)

REVIEW

- Jesus's death provided a way for all people to come to God. It cleared away the sin that kept us from having an effective relationship with God the Father, for anyone who will *trust in him*. Jesus's death on the cross cleared the way back to the Father.

- Jesus's life and death on the cross redeemed us from the second death and gave us access to the gift of eternal life. We all have to die one day, and there's nothing you or I can do about it. However, we don't have to experience the second death.

- God loves you so much that he will not force you to do anything you don't want to do. It is all up to you: the choice is yours.

Chapter 4
Jesus the Perfect Example

The Word became flesh and made his dwelling among us. We have seen his glory, the glory of the One and Only, who came from the Father, full of grace and truth. (John 1:14)

I need to lay the foundation of the purpose of Jesus's life. You may have heard the statement, "Talk is cheap!" or "Easier said than done!" Chances are you may have said them yourself. But from the Word of God, we can see that Jesus's life demonstrated that he walked the walk and talked the talk!

Remember, earlier I mentioned that we all have a purpose. Well, Jesus had a purpose to fulfill also. His purpose was to become a living sacrifice and our mediator to the Father on our behalf. Webster defines the word *mediator* as "one that mediates between parties at variance." In other words, he goes to the Father on our behalf.

In order for Jesus to become that mediator, he had to go through the same things we go through today. When Jesus came into the world, he came in human form just like us with feelings and emotions.

Hebrews 4:14–15 (NKJV) states:

Seeing then that we have a High Priest who has passed through the heavens, Jesus the Son of God, let us hold fast our confession. For we do not have a High Priest who cannot sympathize with our weaknesses, but was in all points tempted as we are, yet without sin.

I believe that a person is able to relate to other people through their own experiences. How can you tell someone how to overcome a certain type of situation that you've never experienced? How can you tell someone that you can live here on earth without sinning if you could not refrain from sinning yourself? Jesus had to become human in order to gain that experience to fight on our behalf. God the Father is a spirit; he has never been human, and that's the reason why Jesus's life was so important.

Jesus knows every challenge that we face every day. He knows that we fall short of the glory of God, but we have been given grace through his death on the cross. The only requirement we must satisfy to have eternal life is to accept Jesus Christ as our Lord and Savior by repenting from our sin and believing that he died on the cross for our sin and that he was raised from the death three days later and is now seated at the right hand of the Father.

How Much Jesus Loves You

He then began to teach them that the Son of Man must suffer many things and be rejected by the elders, chief priests and teachers of the law, and that he must be killed and after three days rise again. (Mark 8:31)

They were on their way up to Jerusalem, with Jesus leading the way, and the disciples were astonished, while those who followed were afraid. Again he took the Twelve aside and told them what was going to happen to him. "We are going up to Jerusalem," he said, "and the Son of Man will be betrayed to the chief priests and teachers of the law. They will condemn him to death and will hand him over to the Gentiles, who will mock him and spit on him, flog him and kill him. Three days later he will rise." (Mark 10:32–34)

It is my belief Jesus spoke to his disciples about what he had to endure to let them know that, when this happened, they were not to worry because it was his destiny. It also showed them that his laying down his life for us was his choice, not because he was forced into it.

If Jesus had never spoken about his death with his disciples in such detail, when it did take place, they would have had a different outlook on the situation.

They would have blamed Judas for Jesus's death. Although Judas did play a vital role in the death of Jesus, you must remember Jesus was born to die for our sins.

Jesus knew what was going to happen to him, and he was still willing to lay down his life for people who didn't love or believe him. That shows how much he loves you and me.

The greatest example of love is the decision to lay down your life for people who don't love you. You might be willing to lay down your life for your parents, your children, or maybe a family member.

However, I'd bet that you would not be willing to lay down your life for a stranger or someone who hates you.

Love is a choice. You have a choice to love someone. We utilize the word *love* when we should be using *like*, because most of us love people conditionally. As long as you do what I say and don't get on my nerves, I will love you, but if you mess up, I'm out of here.

God desires us to love him unconditionally just as his son loves us unconditionally. One thing I love about my Lord and Savior and God my Father is that they never require anything from us that they haven't demonstrated first.

Let me be transparent for a moment because I really want you to understand how much Jesus loves you. I was raised by my grandmother "Essie," and during the time when I first started living with her, I felt like no one loved me.

I felt empty, which caused me to put up guards in my life. I was not willing to give my heart to anyone because of my past hurts.

My grandmother loved me past my pain; she loved me when I did wrong and demonstrated it not by words but by actions.

The love she demonstrated changed my life; my focus was to return the love shown by her. I didn't obey her in order that she wouldn't get mad. I obeyed her because I loved her, and I wanted to demonstrate that love in my actions.

Jesus not only told people that God our Father loves us by sending him to die for our sins. He took it a step further by laying down his life for you and me. How can you not love someone who loved you first?

Chapter 5

Not My Will, but Your Will Be Done

Then Jesus went with his disciples to a place called Gethsemane, and he said to them, "Sit here while I go over there and pray." He took Peter and the two sons of Zebedee along with him, and he began to be sorrowful and troubled. Then he said to them, "My soul is overwhelmed with sorrow to the point of death. Stay here and keep watch with me."

Going a little farther, he fell with his face to the ground and prayed, *"My Father, if it is possible, may this cup be taken from me. Yet not as I will, but as you will."*

Then he returned to his disciples and found them sleeping. "Could you men not keep watch with me for one hour?" he asked Peter. "Watch and pray so that you will not fall into temptation. The spirit is willing, but the body is weak."

He went away a second time and prayed, "My Father, if it is not possible for this cup to be taken away unless I drink it, may your will be done." (Matthew 26:36–42, NIV APP)

An angel from heaven appeared to him and strengthened him. And being in anguish, he prayed more earnestly, and his sweat was like drops of blood falling to the ground.

When he rose from prayer and went back to the disciples, he found them asleep, exhausted from sorrow." (Luke 22:43–45, NIV APP)

Wikepedia Encyclopedia states the following: Hematidrosis (also called hematohidrosis) He-ma-ti-drosis is a very rare condition in which a human being sweats blood. It may occur when a person is suffering extreme levels of stress, for example facing his or her own death.[2]

During this point in Jesus's life, right before his arrest, he battled this terrible time leading up to his death. Jesus became so sorrowful that God sent an angel to strengthen him. Although Jesus already knew he would have to go this route, he still faced all the human emotions, but in the end truly accepted his mission.

Going a little farther, he fell to the ground and prayed that if possible the hour might pass from him. *"Abba, Father," he said, "everything is possible for you. Take this cup from me. Yet not what I will, but what you will." (Mark 14:35–36)*

I've had the opportunity to live in different countries around the world. I've talked to people of different faiths, and what they can't get past is Jesus being the Son of God.

They want to argue that Jesus can't be the Son of God because he is human. Jesus being human was the key because he had to become a sacrifice, and a spirit can't be put to death by man.

As the Son of God resided on this earth in human form, all his emotions and feelings made his sacrifice that much more important. If an alien couldn't feel pain or be killed, would that alien being flogged, spit on, kicked, beaten, and nailed to a cross mean anything? No, I don't think it would have the same impact as a human doing it by his own free will.

You have been created to complete what God designed you for, and there will be times in your life when you experience some of the same emotions Jesus felt in the garden of Gethsemane. My question for you is "How will you respond?"

Thank You for Pushing Me

Then Jesus returned to the disciples and said to them, "Are you still sleeping and resting? Look, the hour is near, and the Son of Man is betrayed into the hands of sinners. Rise, let us go! Here comes my betrayer!"

While he was still speaking, Judas, one of the Twelve, arrived. With him was a large crowd armed with swords and clubs, sent from the chief priests and the elders of the people. Now the betrayer had arranged a signal with them: "The one I kiss is the man; arrest him." Going at once to Jesus, Judas said, "Greetings, Rabbi!" and kissed him.

Jesus replied, "Friend, do what you came for."

Then the men stepped forward, seized Jesus and arrested him. With that, one of Jesus' companions reached for his sword, drew it out and struck the servant of the high priest, cutting off his ear.

"Put your sword back in its place," Jesus said to him, "for all who draw the sword will die by the sword. Do you think I cannot call on my Father, and he will at once put at my disposal more than twelve legions of angels? But how then would the Scriptures be fulfilled that say it must happen in this way?" (Matthew 26:45-54, NIV APP)

How many people do you know who will face a situation beforehand, knowing they will be betrayed by their "friend," in order to achieve the goal and walk out the destiny God has prepared for them? This man Judas walked daily with Jesus, saw the signs and miracles he performed, but still allowed the devil to use him to betray the Son of God.

Did you see Jesus's character and how he handled the situation? Although Peter responded with anger in an attempt to protect Jesus, by cutting off the ear of one of the servants of the high priest, Jesus said no. He condemned this act, for he already knew the route established for him and that the Scriptures had to be fulfilled. Even Jesus had a choice, but he chose obedience and honored the Father instead of forsaking the cross.

Has there ever been a time in your life when you felt betrayed? How did you respond under that type of adversity? Our natural reaction takes no account of the truth that God will turn around what is meant for evil in our life to work in our favor. There are seasons in our lives when we must grow and trust God's plan, and he will allow a situation like this to occur for us to exercise our faith and propel us onto our next level.

The enemy seduced Judas into betraying Jesus, but he did not realize this adversity was pushing Jesus into his divine destiny. You can apply this to your life also. Instead of getting back at the person who betrayed you, instead thank God for allowing that situation to push you into your destiny.

God knows that we are only human, and while he was on earth he experienced our weakness. Althrough he did not fall short from the glory of God. ***Hebrews 4:14-15 states, Seeing then that we have a High Priest who has passed through the heavens, Jesus the Son of God, let us hold fast our confession. For we do not have a High Priest who cannot sympathize with our weaknesses, but was in all points tempted as we are, yet without sin.*** That's why I believe he allows situations in our lives: to push us into our divine destiny. You may be wondering what I'm talking about.

Let's say for example that you asked God to give you an idea that will open up a better financial situation in your life. During your prayer time the Holy Spirit told you to start a business. Please be aware when the Holy Spirit speak to you he does it in your own voice. A year goes by since the Holy Spirit told you to start your own business. However, during this period you aren't unemployed, and you have a job that pays the bills.

You go to God asking what you should do, and the Holy Spirit is telling you to leave your job. However, you say to yourself, I must not have heard God correctly because he wouldn't tell me to leave a job that pays my bills.

You continue praying and thanking God in faith for your new opportunity. A month later your employer relocates to a different city, so they give you a severance package and fire you.

Instead of blaming God for losing that job you need to recall your prayers and view your employer's relocation as pushing you into your destiny. Without the move, you wouldn't have ever started the company God told you to start over a year ago.

Walking the Walk
(Actions Speaking Louder than Words)

Those who had arrested Jesus took him to Caiaphas, the high priest, where the teachers of the law and the elders had assembled ...

The chief priests and the whole Sanhedrin were looking for false evidence against Jesus so that they could put him to death. But they did not find any, though many false witnesses came forward.

Finally two came forward and declared, "This fellow said, "I am able to destroy the temple of God and rebuild it in three days."

Then the high priest stood up and said to Jesus, "Are you not going to answer? What is this testimony that these men are bringing against you?" But Jesus remained silent. (Matthew 26:57, 59–63)

Matthew 26:67–68 states, "Then they spit in his face and struck him with their fists. Others slapped him and said, 'Prophesy to us, Christ. Who hit you?'" Now, since Caiaphas could not find fault in Jesus to put him to death, they then took Jesus to Pilate.

> *Pilate asked Jesus,*
> *"Are you the king of the Jews?"*
> *"Yes, it is as you say," Jesus replied.*
> *When Jesus was accused by the chief priests and the elders, he gave no answer. Then Pilate asked him, "Don't you hear the testimony they are bringing against you?" But Jesus made no reply, not even to a single charge—to the great amazement of the governor. (Matthew 27:11–14)*

Now it was Pilate's custom during the feast to release a prisoner chosen by the public. During that time he had in custody a prisoner named Barabbas, so he asked the crowd which prisoner they wanted him to release. Please keep in mind that Barabbas was a notorious prisoner. He had been convicted for killing, and the crowd chose to release Barabbas instead of Jesus.

Thank God, for if they had chosen Jesus to be released, he would not have gone to the cross, and we would have been lost. Pilate then asked the crowd what did they want him to do with Jesus, and they all answered, "Crucify him!" Pilate knew that Jesus had done no wrong, and he asked the crowd "Why should I crucify him? What crime has he committed?" But the crowd shouted louder and louder, "Crucify him!"

When Pilate saw that he was getting nowhere, but that instead an uproar was starting, he took water and washed his hands in front of the crowd. "I am innocent of this man's blood," he said. "It is your responsibility!"

All the people answered, "Let his blood be on us and on our children!" Then he released Barabbas to them. But he had Jesus flogged, and handed him over to be crucified.

Then the governor's soldiers took Jesus into the Praetorium and gathered the whole company of soldiers around him. They stripped him and put a scarlet robe on him, and then twisted together a crown of thorns and set it on his head. They put a staff in his right hand and knelt in front of him and mocked him. "Hail, king of the Jews!" they said. They spit on him, and took the staff and struck him on the head again and again. After they had mocked him, they took off the robe and

put his own clothes on him. Then they led him away to crucify him. (Matthew 27:24–31, NIV APP)

During this time a man to be crucified was made to carry his own cross. While Jesus was carrying his cross, they arrived to a place called Golgotha. There they offered Jesus wine to drink, mixed with gall; but after tasting it, he refused to drink it.

You may be wondering, Why did Jesus refuse to take a drink? Well, let me shed a little light on this situation. Gall is generally understood to be a narcotic that was used to deaden pain. Jesus refused to deaden the pain he was experiencing. He would suffer fully conscious and with a clear mind.

When they came to the place called the Skull, there they crucified him, along with the criminals—one on his right, the other on his left. Jesus said, "Father, forgive them, for they do not know what they are doing." And they divided up his clothes by casting lots. (Luke 23:34–35, NIV APP)

One of the criminals who hung there hurled insults at him: "Aren't you the Christ? Save yourself and us!"

But the other criminal rebuked him. "Don't you fear God," he said, "since you are under the same sentence? We are punished justly, for we are getting what our deeds deserve. But this man has done nothing wrong."

Then he said, "Jesus, remember me when you come into your kingdom. Jesus answered him, "I tell you the

truth, today you will be with me in paradise." (Luke 23:39–43, NIV APP)

Matthew 27:36 states it was about the ninth hour (midafternoon) when "Jesus cried out in a loud voice, 'Eloi, Eloi, lama sabachthani?' which means, 'My God, my God, why have you forsaken me?'"

I want you to be aware that Jesus was not crying to God the Father asking him why he had left him. God promises us in his Word that he will never leave us.

The LORD himself goes before you and will be with you; he will never leave you nor forsake you. Do not be afraid; do not be discouraged. (Deuteronomy 31:8, NIV APP)

When Jesus cried out in anguish "My God, my God, why have you forsaken me?" he was actually quoting Psalm 22:1–8:

My God, my God, why have you forsaken me?
Why are you so far from saving me,
so far from the words of my groaning?
O my God, I cry out by day, but you do not answer,
by night, and am not silent.
Yet you are enthroned as the Holy One;
you are the praise of Israel.
In you our fathers put their trust;
they trusted and you delivered them.
They cried to you and were saved;
in you they trusted and were not disappointed.

But I am a worm and not a man,
  scorned by men and despised by the people.
All who see me mock me;
  they hurl insults, shaking their heads:
"He trusts in the LORD;
  let the LORD rescue him.
Let him deliver him,
  since he delights in him.

Matthew 27:50 states that "when Jesus had cried out again in a loud voice, he gave up his spirit." Jesus' mission was complete! Don't you want to accomplish what God created you to accomplish? I don't know about you, but when I depart this world I want to leave knowing that I completed my assignment.

Pause & Reflect

You were created for a purpose. You are not an accident or a mistake. Your mother and father may not have planned for you to enter this world on that special day, but I have good news for you. God's plan overshadowed theirs. God created you to accomplish something great for the kingdom of God.

The trials you may be facing in your life now are preparing you to take your rightful place and fill the position he created you for. I'm here to tell you that no one else can do what God created you to accomplish. No one can reach the people God created you to reach. You are unique, and that is the way God wanted it. During those times of testing, remember that in the garden of Gethsemane Jesus didn't want to go to the cross, but nevertheless he said, "Not my will be done, but Father, your will be done."

REVIEW

- Jesus's purpose was to become a living sacrifice and our mediator to the Father on our behalf.

- Jesus has now become our high priest, since he can understand our weaknesses. During his earthly ministry he "was in all points tempted as we are, yet without sin" (Hebrews 4:15, NKJV).

- There are seasons in our lives when we must grow and trust God's plan. He will allow situations to occur so we will exercise our faith and and be ushered onto our next level.

III. The Burial

Chapter 6
The Burial of Your Old Man

I discussed your reward which is on the other side of your situation and reviewed several examples. Now that you know what is waiting for you on the other side of your problem, we must discuss what is required from you and how to achieve that relationship that God desires with you.

God only has one requirement that you must meet to inherit the kingdom of God and receive all the promises he has in store for you. That is simply to put him first in every area of your life. You do this by laying yourself aside and accepting his way of living for your life. You must lay aside that sinful nature, repent of your sins, and accept Jesus as your Lord and Savior.

You may say that God loves you no matter what you do. Yes, he does. However, he does not love your sinful nature, and that sinful nature is what separates you from the Father. I have good news for you. God knows that our sinful nature contributes to our downfall, and that was the reason he sent his Son, Jesus, to die for our sins.

Just as man is destined to die once, and after that to face judgment, so Christ was sacrificed once to take away the sins of many people; and he will appear a second time, not to bear sin, but to bring salvation to those who are waiting for him. (Hebrews 9:27–28)

You may be saying, "I'm not a bad person! I don't go around stealing, cheating, or killing people. I treat everyone nice, and I also go to church, so how can I be a sinner?"

To some who were confident of their own righteousness and looked down on everybody else, Jesus told this parable:

"Two men went up to the temple to pray, one a Pharisee and the other a tax collector. The Pharisee stood up and prayed about himself: 'God, I thank you that I am not like other men—robbers, evildoers, adulterers—or even like this tax collector. I fast twice a week and give a tenth of all I get.'

"But the tax collector stood at a distance. He would not even look up to heaven, but beat his breast and said 'God, have mercy on me, a sinner.'

"I tell you that this man, rather than the other, went home justified before God. For everyone who exalts himself will be humbled, and he who humbles himself will be exalted." (Luke 18:9–14)

What this means is that no man can be justified before God through his own acts. What God seeks from us is a humble spirit and not a prideful one. You may be saying you can't live the life that is required to have a relationship with God or that being a Christian is nothing but following a bunch of rules and that it's too hard for you to do. This walk with God is filled with challenges, but remember, God is always available to help you if you acknowledge him, and by faith you will overcome them all.

The apostle Paul was a man who persecuted Christians but, after receiving Jesus as his Lord and Savior, dedicated his life to spreading the gospel that he used to fight against. Due to the relationship Paul had established with Jesus, he trusted him totally. However, in his early ministry he struggled in different areas in his life just as we do, but he did not quit fighting the good fight of faith.

We know that the law is spiritual; but I am unspiritual, sold as a slave to sin. I do not understand what I do. For what I want to do I do not do, but what I hate I do. And if I do what I do not want to do, I agree that the law is good. As it is, is no longer I myself who do it, but it is sin living in me. I know that nothing good lives in me, that is, in my sinful nature. For I have the desire to do what is good, but I cannot carry it out. For what I do is not the good I want to do; no, the evil I do not want to do—this I keep on doing. Now if I do what I do not want to do, it is no longer I who do it, but it is sin living in me what does it.

So I find this law at work: When I want to do good, evil is right there with me. For in my inner being I delight in God's law; but I see another law at work in the members of my body, waging war against the law of my mind and making me a prisoner of the law of sin at work within my members. What a wretched man I am!

Who will rescue me from this body of death? Thanks be to God—through Jesus Christ our Lord!

So then, I myself in my mind am a slave to God's law, but in the sinful nature a slave to the law of sin. (Romans 7:14–25)

Paul looked to Jesus Christ, the author and finisher of his faith (see Hebrews 12:2), to overcome all obstacles that he faced. God gave him the grace to win! During Jesus's ministry, you'll notice, he not only preached about the consequences of sin but also taught us how to live and how to treat one another. Jesus's life was the perfect example for us to emulate. Jesus' actions coincide with his words, and that is what God desires from you and me.

In the garden of Gethsemane, Jesus had the power to call a legion of angels to his defense, but he didn't! Why? Because he loves you so much that he was willing to go through those three terrible days, giving you a way to back to the Father.

Many people utilize the word *love* and have no idea what love truly means. Love is a choice. You choose to love someone, and when you truly love someone, it is unconditional. The problem with us is that we have no idea how to truly love others. We love people as long as it benefits us. Our love is conditional, and the love of Jesus and the Father for us is unconditional.

Jesus loves you so much that he died for you when you didn't even acknowledge him. God loves us so much that he sent his Son, Jesus, to die for us so we would have a right to eternal life. The way to be free from sin is to trust Jesus Christ to take all of your sin away. You must stand firm in the gospel, putting all your confidence in Jesus alone to forgive your sins and to make you right with God.

Let me explain something to you. God could have created us to love him unconditionally. He could have made us obey, but if that was so, how would he know that we truly love him? When you truly love someone, it is not based on what they can do for you. You will put them first and even place their feelings above your own. That is true love, and that is what the Father shows us every day. How can you not love those who put you before themselves?

I pray and have faith that if you have read this far, you have opened your heart and accepted Jesus Christ as your Lord and Savior. Accepting Jesus as your Lord and Savior is a very big accomplishment, but now it's time for the burial of your old man.

You may be wondering what I mean by the burial of your old man. When you accepted Jesus Christ as your Lord and Savior, you were spiritually reborn. You are now a new creature.

> *Therefore, if anyone is in Christ, he is a new creation; the old has gone, the new has come! All this is from God, who reconciled us to himself through Christ and gave us the ministry of reconciliation. (2 Corinthians 5:17–18)*

You must now turn away from your "old way" of living. What I mean by that is things of the flesh that are contradicting to the Word of God. We will take a closer look at this in the next section.

STRONGHOLDS
Hindrances to Your Spiritual Growth

In this section I will be using the word *stronghold* to stand for things in your life that will hinder your spiritual growth. Some examples of strongholds are drugs, alcoholism, sexual sins, adultery, homosexuality, pride, jealousy, unforgiveness, or anything that goes against the Word of God. You may be thinking some of the examples I listed aren't sin, but let me be very clear: *Anything* that goes against the Word of God or you place before God is a sin.

> *You shall have no other gods before Me. (Exodus 20:3, NKJV)*

> *Where your treasure is, there your heart will be also. (Matthew 6:21, NKJV)*

> *No one can serve two masters; for either he will hate the one and love the other, or else he will be loyal to the one and despise the other. You cannot serve God and mammon. (Matthew 6:23, NKJV)*

It is very important to me that you understand if you don't take time out to address these issues in your life, they will hinder your spiritual growth. No matter how big or small you think they are, through Christ you can overcome them.

I almost didn't put this section in the book because I didn't want to overwhelm you. However, I had to be obedient to the Holy Spirit and provide you with the information so you can know what you are dealing with.

My people are destroyed for lack of knowledge.
Because you have rejected knowledge,
I also will reject you from being priest for Me;
because you have forgotten the law of your God,
I also will forget your children. (Hosea 4:6, NKJV)

Perhaps not all strongholds that you may encounter have been created by your own doing but came down through your blood line. You have probably heard some people justify the things they do because their parents have similar tendencies. Many times their logic is correct if these actions have been passed down through their generations.

The LORD passed before him and proclaimed.
"The LORD, the LORD God, merciful and gracious,
longsuffering, and abounding in goodness and truth,
keeping mercy for thousands, forgiving iniquity and
transgression and sin, by no means clearing the guilty,
visiting the iniquity of the fathers upon the children
and the children's children to the third and the fourth
generation. (Exodus 34:6–7, NKJV)

How can you overcome these things? The sins of our ancestors passed down through generations can greatly affect our lives. These doorways of inheritance must be closed by prayer, confession, and the cleansing power of the blood of Jesus Christ.

Now on the twenty-fourth day of this month the children
of Israel were assembled with fasting, in sackcloth,

and with dust on their heads. Then those of Israelite lineage separated themselves from all foreigners; and they stood and confessed their sins and the iniquities of their fathers. (Nehemiah 9:1–2, NKJV)

I will now discuss other open doorways in your life that can create strongholds in your life and hinder your spiritual growth. What are doorways? Doorways are created by sin and give Satan legal ground in your life, and this holds true for believers as well. The opening of these doorways involves your participation in sin even if you are committing sin in your ignorance.

Shall we sin because we are not under law but under grace? Certainly not! Do you not know that to whom you present yourselves slaves to obey, you are that one's slaves whom you obey, whether of sin leading to death, or of obedience leading to righteousness? (Romans 6:15–16, NKJV)

Many people are not willing to accept Jesus as their Lord and Savior because their will and mind are bound by the Enemy through an open doorway in their life, past or present. Many have accepted Jesus as their Lord and Savior but later found themselves not growing spiritually, basically stuck with no clue of the reason why.

The god of this age has blinded the minds of unbelievers, so that they cannot see the light of the gospel of the glory of Christ, who is the image of God. (2 Corinthians 4:4)

There are numerous ways doorways in your spiritual life can be opened. Some of them are the Eastern religions (e.g., Masonic oaths); the occult arts, including horoscope reading or visiting fortunetellers, tea leaf readers, or palm readers (no matter how brief the encounters); and being a victim to any type of sexual attack.

In 1996 I joined the Masonic Lodge and became a Mason. I began to admire this organization during my youth because I saw Masons doing a lot of charity work, and they seemed influential in the community. I thought to myself it would be great to belong to a group with so much influence and popularity. At that time, I didn't realize that not everything that appears good on the outside is good. Satan is very cunning and knows that you would never serve him as he is, so he utilizes tricks to deceive you. However, as children of the Most High God, we can overcome any trick Satan may try to use against us.

Dear friends, do not believe every spirit, but test the spirits to see whether they are from God, because many false prophets have gone out into the world. This is how you can recognize the Spirit of God: Every spirit that acknowledges that Jesus Christ has come in the flesh is from God, but every spirit that does not acknowledge Jesus is not from God. This is the spirit of the antichrist, which you have heard is coming and even now is already in the world.

You, dear children, are from God and have overcome them, because the one who is in you is greater than the one who is in the world. (1 John 4:1–4)

During the process of becoming a Mason, I took part in a lot of rituals, thinking that it was just something you do to become a part of this fraternity of brothers. Years after becoming part of this organization I started hearing stories about this fraternity. People were saying this was a religion, and as a person who was raised in church all my life, I debated this matter all the time. I would tell people that I was saved and loved God the Father and believed Jesus is the Son of God.

Later in my adulthood I decided to conduct research and seek the truth on my own. Through prayer, after looking at the history of the organization and what the ritual practices represented, I realized that I could no longer be associated with this fraternity of brothers. My links to this organization created strongholds in my life that hindered me from growing spiritually. I mention this to illustrate that sometimes people open doorways unaware, and that's why this section is so important.

> *Let no one be found among you who sacrifices his son or daughter in the fire, who practices divination or sorcery, interprets omens, engages in witchcraft, or cast spells, or who is a medium or spiritist or who consults the dead. Anyone who does these things is detestable to the LORD, and because of these detestable practices the LORD your God will drive out those nations before you. (Deuteronomy 18:10–12)*

You must also be aware that any dealing with Satan opens a doorway in your life, and it doesn't matter if you are a Christian or non-Christian. Satan doesn't care, because the sin in your life gives him legal grounds to operate. However, the good news is that you can put that sin under Jesus's blood and ask for forgiveness, and God is faithful and just to forgive you (see 1 John 1:9). The sins you have committed in your life will be wiped away as if you had never committed them. When you ask for forgiveness from all your sins, this action removes the sin, which then revokes Satan's legal right in your life.

I want you to be aware after you repent from your sins, the devil will still try to bring them back to your memory. He will tell you that God didn't forgive you; he doesn't forgive that type of sin. When Satan tries to convince you that you weren't forgiven, I want you to repeat these words: "Get behind me, Satan, for it is written that if I repent with a sincere heart, God is faithful and just to forgive me from all sin."

I started this project more than two years ago and actually completed it in the beginning of 2009. When you are walking with the Lord, he will direct everything including when to release the information to the public. As I complete this section, I'm living overseas in a Muslim country where it is illegal for Muslims to convert to Christianity. I've had the opportunity to watch Muslims interact in their daily lives and see their ritualistic practices.

In this country most Muslims are dedicated to their prayer time. The call for prayers goes out several times a day on loudspeakers which can be heard throughout the city. Because the primary dialects are French and Arabic, I don't understand what is actually being said, but I do see people gather to pray *one prayer* at the *same time* in *one accord*.

There is a spiritual law in this that I want you to be aware of. Unless we are vigilant, the Enemy will use spiritual laws against us which will keep us from coming to the full knowledge of Christ Jesus. Spiritual laws, when applied correctly, serve the just as well as the unjust.

They said to one another, "Come, let us make bricks and bake them thoroughly." They had brick for stone, and they had asphalt for mortar. And they said, "Come, let us build ourselves a city, and a tower whose top is in the heavens; let us make a name for ourselves, lest we be scattered abroad over the face of the whole earth." But the LORD came down to see the city and the tower which the sons of men had built. And the LORD said, "Indeed the people are one and they all have one language, and this is what they begin to do; now nothing that they propose to do will be withheld from them." (Genesis 11:3–6, NJKV)

As you grow in your spiritual walk, you will learn about speaking the Word of God into the atmosphere. This planet and everything that exists was created by God. He created all things by speaking them into existence, and this principle holds true today for us as well.

The Spirit of God was hovering over the face of the waters. Then God said, "Let there be light"; and there was light. (Genesis 1:2–3, NKJV)

The entire first chapter of Genesis describes how God created everything on this planet by speaking into the atmosphere. This principle is also mentioned in the book of Proverbs more directly: *"Death and life are in the power of the tongue, and those who love it will eat its fruit" (Proverbs 18:21, NKJV).*

When you come together on anything, in one mind, one speech, and one spirit, nothing can be withheld from you no matter what that thing may be. The devil knows this, and he utilizes this to keep Christians defeated in certain areas of their lives. In my opinion one of the greatest deceptions used by Satan is the creation of church denominations, which keeps Christians separated each week. It keeps Christians divided so we can never come to one accord to do the great work God planned for us. As long as the Body of Christ remains divided through church denominations, we can never truly come together as children of the Most High God, achieve greatness, and live as God intended for us to live, "on earth as it is in heaven" (see Matthew 6:10).

I mentioned this example of being in one accord so you can see how being in one accord for things that are *not* the will of God can produce strongholds in your life. It is my desire for you to be wise and have knowledge of the devil's schemes as he will tempt to trip you up in your walk with God. These things should not be ignored because spiritual warfare is a reality whether you think it is true or not.

Put on the full armor of God so that you can take your stand against the devil's schemes. For our struggle is not against flesh and blood, but against the rulers, against the authorities, against the powers of this dark world and against the spiritual forces of evil in the heavenly realms. Therefore put on the full armor of God, so that when the day of evil comes, you may be able to stand your ground, and after you have done everything, to stand. (Ephesians 6:11–13)

Pause & Reflect

God has made available many promises in his Word. God has also given us the opportunity to receive the gift of eternal life, but there is one requirement that you must do to gain access to the promises of God, and that is accept Jesus as your Lord and Savior

Accepting Jesus Christ as your Lord and Savior is just the first step. Next you will begin developing a relationship, getting to know the Father, and learning his ways. You are not expected to live a perfect life, but you are expected to continue fighting the good fight of faith. Don't be afraid of making a mistake, and don't give up when you fall.

To accept Jesus as your Lord and Savior, you must believe he died and God raised him from the dead three days later, and it truly requires faith. Now if you believe and are ready to receive him in your heart, I want you to say this prayer:

Father God, I am a sinner, and I ask you to forgive me for my sins. I thank you for sending your Son, Jesus, to die for me when I didn't acknowledge you. I thank you for loving me when I did not love you. I ask you to come into my life and save me. I accept Jesus as my Lord and Savior. I believe that he died on the cross just for me and that you raised him from the dead three days later. Thank you for saving me, in Jesus's name, amen!

Welcome to the family of God!

REVIEW

- God only has one requirement that you must meet to inherit the kingdom of God and receive all the promises he has in store for you, and that is to put him first in every area of your life.

- In life you will face many challenges. But remember, God is always available to help you if you acknowledge him, and by faith you will overcome them all.

- The burial of your old man must take place in order for you to walk in your divine destiny.

- Any sin in your life gives Satan legal grounds to enter and disrupt your life.

- Be smart by learning from your past mistakes, and take it one step further by learning from others' past mistakes.

- Protect yourself from the devil's traps by putting on the whole armor of God

- The devil will try to deceive you by telling you that you weren't forgiven.

- Don't give up, continue fighting the good fight, and you can successful bury your old man.

IV. The Resurrection

Chapter 7
The New Life

In this section I will discuss the beginning of your Christian walk. I want you to know that I may not cover every question you may have, but I encourage you to get involved in a Bible-based church because they will be able to assist you in this growth process.

As I stated earlier, although you are now a Christian, that doesn't mean you will never have any more problems. This is a major misconception among new believers. Once they get saved, they seem to think that everything should go their way and simply fall into place. In fact, now that you are a Christian, your adversary, the devil, is going to attack you more aggressively in an attempt to cause you to lose faith in the Word of God and to think that this lifestyle doesn't work. The same problems that unbelievers go through, Christians also go through. However, our lifestyle requires us to apply biblical principles (which always work when applied correctly) that will enable us to live victorious lives in Christ Jesus.

To be successful in this Christian walk, you must live by faith. You must exercise your faith daily; that is the only way it will grow.

Without faith it is impossible to please God, because anyone who comes to him must believe that he exists and that he rewards those who earnestly seek him. (Hebrews 11:6)

This Christian walk is a faith walk, but you must also remember that you live and operate on this earth. Everything you do in this life involves cause and effect. For example, if you steal from someone and ask God to forgive you, he is faithful and just to forgive you, but you are still going to have to suffer the consequences of your actions down here on this earth.

I feel this is important for you to understand because you need to learn to depend on God. I have heard people say they are trusting God and are "standing in faith" but display no action corresponding with what they are believing God for. For instance, someone says she is "standing in faith" for a job but has never gone out to look or apply for a job. She must think the job is going to automatically show up on her doorstep with no action on her part at all.

Yes, she may have been utilizing her faith in this situation by believing God would supply her needs, but this is totally one-sided. She forgot one important part, and that is action. Her part of it would have been to go out and apply for a job and believe God for favor with the employer. I'm here to tell you that faith without works is dead. Where are your works?

What does it profit, my brethren, if someone says he has faith but does not have works? Can faith save him? If a brother or sister is naked and destitute of daily food, and one of you says to them, "Depart in peace, be warmed and filled," but you do not give them the things which are needed for the body, what does it profit? Thus also faith by itself, if it does not have works, is dead. But someone will say, You have faith, and I have works. Show me your faith without your works, and I will show you my faith by my works. You believe that there is one God. You do well. Even the demons believe—and tremble! But do you want to know, O foolish man, that faith without works is dead? (James 2:14–20, NKJV)

God is a supernatural being, and he handles the "supernatural" part, but you are responsible for the natural. The Holy Spirit in you is always available to teach you what you can do in your own power and by faith expect to receive from the Father. God created us to rule over this earth, the birds of the air, and the fish in the sea. It is not God's responsibility to rule the earth; he has given that responsibility to you.

The Birth of Your New Man

Now that you have been born again, you must start operating as God has established for you by gaining access to the Kingdom of God.

> *Jesus declared, "I tell you the truth, no one can see the kingdom of God unless he is born again."*
>
> *"How can a man be born when he is old?" Nicodemus asked. "Surely he cannot enter a second time into his mother's womb to be born!"*
>
> *Jesus answered. "I tell you the truth, no one can enter the kingdom of God unless he is born of water and the Spirit. Flesh gives birth to flesh, but the Spirit gives birth to spirit." (John 3:3–6)*

Most Christians get stuck right at the very moment of their salvation and never get to the place of operating on this earth with dominion and power. Most Christians believe that after accepting Jesus, they are finished, and they live their lives "waiting" to receive their rewards when they get to heaven.

That statement is only partially true; the Christian's reward for righteous living and accepting Jesus as Lord and Savior is eternal life, and that new life begins immediately here on earth. And the Word of God has given us the keys to living that life, and that is seeking the kingdom of God in every area of our lives. Everything that we will ever need has already been provided; we just have to learn how to access it and lay hold of it.

I tell you that not even Solomon in all his splendor was dressed like one of these. If that is how God clothes the grass of the field, which is here today and tomorrow is thrown into the fire, will he not much more clothe you, O you of little faith? So do not worry, saying, "What shall we eat?" or "What shall we drink?" or "What shall we wear?" For the pagans run after all these things, and your heavenly Father knows that you need them. But seek first his kingdom and his righteousness, and all these things will be given to you as well. (Matthew 6:29–33)

The kingdom of God is the government of God. Any government has rules and laws that we must abide by in order receive all the benefits that particular government has to offer in order to operate effectively. Jesus's life was based on the principles of the kingdom of God, and as you study, you will see the kingdom of God revealed.

I'm here to tell you that after you have made Jesus Christ your Lord and Savior, your life truly has just begun. It is now time for you to live the life God purposed for you and let your life be an example for others to emulate, the way Jesus's life set the example for us to follow. We should live our lives as Jesus did. How do we accomplish this task of living our lives as Jesus did? Well, as I have stated many times before, you need to get into the Word of God, study the Scriptures for yourself, and begin to examine Jesus's life and learn how he responded to different situations. This dedication and spending time in the Word will be a learning process, but you must determine that this is what you need to do in order to grow in your own walk with God.

The Holy Spirit within You

One of our greatest gifts God gives us once we are born again is the empowerment of the Holy Spirit who dwells within us. Before Jesus went back to the Father, he promised that we would not be left alone. He promised to send us help.

> *On one occasion, while he was eating with them, he gave them this command: "Do not leave Jerusalem, but wait for the gift my Father promised, which you have heard me speak about. For John baptized with water, but in a few days you will be baptized with the Holy Spirit." (Acts 1:4–5)*

To walk in full authority and complete our assignments, we must have the Holy Spirit dwelling within us, because it is impossible to live as Christ did without the Holy Spirit. Jesus knew this and therefore instructed his disciples to wait in Jerusalem until they received the Holy Spirit. Without the Holy Spirit, they would have been limited in their own power in advancing the kingdom of God.

When you study the ministry of Jesus, you'll learn that he did not start his ministry until he was filled and led by the Holy Spirit. Jesus was baptized by John the Baptist so that the Scriptures would be fulfilled. He then went into the wilderness for forty days of fasting and praying. During this time Jesus was given instruction, strengthened, and empowered by the Holy Spirit to walk out his destiny on the earth.

We should take this example from Jesus and do the same thing. Once you've taken the first step of accepting Jesus as your

Lord and Savior, you must acquire the tool needed to complete your assignment, and that tool is the empowerment of the Holy Spirit. You may be asking, "How do I receive the Holy Spirit?" The only thing you must do is ask and receive him by faith because he has already been promised to you. Luke 11:13 says, "If you, then, though you are evil, know how to give good gifts to your children, how much more will your Father in heaven give the Holy Spirit to those who ask him!"

You may ask yourself another question: "What purpose does the Holy Spirit serve in my life?" The Holy Spirit is capable of helping you in anything that you may be lacking in your life.

The Comforter (Counselor, Helper, Intercessor, Advocate, Strengthener, Standby), the Holy Spirit, Who the Father will send in My name [in My place to represent Me and act on my behalf], He will teach you all things. And He will cause you to recall (will remind you of, bring to your remembrance) everything I have told you. (John 14:26, Amplified)

The Holy Spirit will be an encourager when you feel that you can't make it anymore. He is capable of warning you of approaching danger. Anything that you will ever need to know, the Holy Spirit knows, and he is able to reveal it to your spirit.

I also want you to be aware that the Holy Spirit provides different spiritual gifts. There are a variety of gifts, but they all work together for the glory of God and to further his kingdom here on earth.

There are different kinds of gifts, but the same Spirit. There are different kinds of service, but the same Lord. There are different kinds of working, but the same God works all of them in all men.

Now to each one the manifestation of the Spirit is given for the common good. To one there is given through the Spirit the message of wisdom, to another the message of knowledge by means of the same Spirit, to another faith by the same Spirit, to another gifts of healing by that one Spirit, to another miraculous powers, to another prophecy, to another distinguishing between spirits, to another speaking in different kinds of tongues, and to still another the interpretation of tongues. All these are the work on one and the same Spirit, and he gives them to each one, just as he determines. (1 Corinthians 12:4–11)

It is very important for you to understand that the Holy Spirit may empower a person with any one or more of numerous gifts. However, you must remember that it's just as he determines. For example, you may have been given the gift of tongues but not the gift of interpretation of tongues. Why am I bringing this to your attention? I want you to understand that your gift is no greater than another gift operating by the Holy Spirit.

All true believers and followers of Jesus Christ are part of the body of Christ. In order for the body to function correctly, it must utilize different parts. No part is more important than another part. Without all the parts working together, the body will not function the way it was designed to function.

The smallest part of the body is a cell, and it is the start of all life. Cells grow in a special way. The center divides in half, and then the cell divides into two cells. The two cells become four, and the four become eight, and so on. There are many different types of cells. Their shape depends on what their job is. Nerve cells have long branches so that messages can be sent through your body. Muscle cells are long and elastic. Cells grow into different types and shapes that your body needs to function. One thing that all these different types of cells have in common is that by themselves they may seem unimportant, but all the different types of cells are needed in order for the body to function correctly.

The eye cannot say to the hand, "I don't need you!" And the head cannot say to the feet, "I don't need you!" On the contrary, those parts of the body that seem to be weaker are indispensable, and the parts that we think are less honorable we treat with special honor. And the parts that are unpresentable are treated with special modesty, while our presentable parts need no special treatment. But God has combined the members of the body and has given greater honor to the parts that lacked it, so that there should be no division in the body, but that its parts should have equal concern for each other. If one part suffers, every part suffers with it; if one part is honored, every part rejoices with it.

Now you are the body of Christ, and each one of you is a part of it. (1 Corinthians 12:21–27)

Regardless of what gifting the Holy Spirit empowers you with, remember that all gifts are equally important in the body of Christ. I'm here to tell you it does not matter what gift the Holy Spirit gives you because all gifts are equally important in the body of Christ. I encourage you to speak life and love into all children of God. Encourage them to walk in their divine destiny and exercise the gift the Holy Spirit has given them because their gift is needed to ensure that the body of Christ is functioning properly.

You may ask yourself another question: "How do I know when the Holy Spirit is talking to me?" The Holy Spirit speaks to your spirit. It will take diligence to learn and become aware of his voice. When he speaks, he will always lead you into peace. Whatever the Holy Spirit tells or instruct you to do will always line up with the Word of God. He will never tell you to do anything that goes against the Word of God because he is the Spirit of God and will only speak what the Father says.

When He, the Spirit of Truth (the Truth-giving Spirit) comes, He will guide you into all the Truth (the whole, full Truth). For He will not speak His own message [on his own authority]; but He will tell whatever He hears [from the Father; He will give the message that has been given to Him], and He will announce and declare to you the things that are to come [that will happen in the future]. (John 16:13, Amplified)

What I love about the Holy Spirit is that he knows me better than I know myself and is always available to pray on my behalf when I don't know what to pray about.

The Spirit helps us in our weakness. We do not know what we ought to pray for, but the Spirit himself intercedes for us with groans that words cannot express. And he who searches our hearts knows the mind of the

Spirit, because the Spirit intercedes for the saints in accordance with God's will. (Romans 8:26–27)

The Holy Spirit is your greatest helper as you fulfill your purpose on this earth. He knows the will of God for your life and will always guide you in the right direction. In your daily time of prayer and studying the Word, the Father will give you instruction and clarity through the Holy Spirit. Begin to acknowledge the presence of the Holy Spirit; he is always available to assist you to complete the will of God in your daily walk.

REVIEW

- The lifestyle of a Christian requires us to apply biblical principles that will enable us to live victorious lives in Christ Jesus.

- To be successful in this Christian walk, you must live by faith. You must exercise your faith daily; that is the only way it will grow.

- This dedication to spending time in the Word will be a learning process, but you must determine that this is what you need to do in order to grow in your own walk with God.

- To walk in full authority and complete our assignments, we must have the Holy Spirit dwelling within us, because it is impossible to live as Christ did without the Holy Spirit.

- The Holy Spirit is always available to teach you what you can't do in your own power. By faith you may expect to receive him from the Father.

Chapter 8
Who Am I?

Once again I would like to welcome you into the family of God!. Now, after accepting Jesus Christ as your Lord and Savior, you have now become one of the co-heirs with Christ. You may wonder what that means to you. Well, it means that all the promises of God that he made available through Christ Jesus are now made available to you. You have been given all the power and authority to reign as kings in life through Christ Jesus.

> *You are all sons of God through faith in Christ Jesus, for all of you who were baptized into Christ have clothed yourselves with Christ. There is neither Jew nor Greek, slave nor free, male nor female, for you are all one in Christ Jesus. If you belong to Christ, then you are Abraham's seed, and heirs according to the promise. (Galatians 3:26–29)*

The Spirit himself testifies with our spirit that we are God's children. Now if we are children, then we are heirs—heirs of God and co-heirs with Christ, if indeed we share in his sufferings in order that we may also share in his glory. (Romans 8:16–17)

The Word of God tells us in Ephesians 2:5–6 that God "made us alive together in Christ (by grace you have been saved), and raised us up together, and made us sit together in the heavenly places in Christ Jesus" (NKJV). This is the position he prepared for us before the foundation of the world.

Now that you know what position you have been granted, let's take a moment to talk about the power and authority that was given to you. You may be wondering why we are discussing this topic and why it is important. I believe that it is important for you to know who you have become. If you truly know who you are, it will affect the way you conduct yourself in your daily life.

Restoring What Was Lost

After you have accepted Jesus Christ as your Lord and Savior, you may look back over your life and see all the mistakes that you made during your time of disobedience. As you reflect over your life, you may feel that you missed out on blessings as well as opportunities that are affecting your life today.

There may be some people in your life that you have mistreated, and you wish you could go back and correct those mistakes. It may be impossible to travel back in time and correct those wrongs, but I have some good news for you. God has the ability and desires to correct those things in your life and place you where he ordained you to be.

> *I will repay you for the years the locusts have eaten—*
> *the great locust and the young locust,*
> *the other locusts and the locust swarm—*
> *my great army that I sent among you.*
> *You will have plenty to eat, until you are full,*
> *and you will praise the name of the LORD your God,*
> *who has worked wonders for you;*
> *never again will my people be shamed. (Joel 2:25–26)*

God, our heavenly Father, loves us, and he loves to see his children happy. God is waiting for you to ask him to right the wrongs in your life, and he is faithful and just to do just as he promised in the book of Joel.

In 2 Kings we read that King Hezekiah had an illness, and he prayed that God would heal him from this illness. During this period God sent Isaiah to Hezekiah to tell him that the Lord would heal him, and he would live. Although Hezekiah had been praying, still, once he received the good news concerning his healing, he still wanted proof.

Hezekiah asked Isaiah "What will be the sign that the Lord will heal me?" (see 2 Kings 20:8). Hezekiah knew God had the power to do all things, but he wanted to make sure that he heard him correctly. Let me explain that there is nothing wrong with asking God to give you a sign that you heard him correctly. There is nothing wrong in verifying your task prior to executing it.

> *Hezekiah had asked Isaiah, "What will be the sign that the LORD will heal me and that I will go up to the temple of the LORD on the third day from now?"*
>
> *Isaiah answered, "This is the LORD's sign to you that the LORD will do what he has promised: Shall the shadow go forward ten steps, or shall it go back ten steps?"*
>
> *"It is a simple matter for the shadow to go forward ten steps," said Hezekiah. "Rather, have it go back ten steps."*
>
> *Then the prophet Isaiah called upon the LORD, and the LORD made the shadow go back the ten steps it had gone down on the stairway of Ahaz. (2 Kings 20:8–11)*

If God physically made the sun's shadow move in reverse, representing that he turned back the time for Hezekiah, I know he is capable of presenting this opportunity to you.

There was a period in my life when my occupation separated me from my family for long periods of time. I knew that God was in control and had a plan for my life. I held on to God's promise that my latter days would be greater than my former years, and the best things God had for my life were ahead of me.

During this period in my life I noticed the strain on my family, and I felt if I didn't do something quickly, I could cause damage that I couldn't repair. Since my separation from my family was job related, there was nothing I could do but quit my job. Since I didn't have another job lined up where my family resided, I had to go to God for help. I prayed that God would restore the time I had lost while I was currently away from my family.

As I continued visiting my family on weekends and holidays, I noticed that my marriage started getting stronger, and my relationship with my daughters was as close as ever. I would like to think that God was turning back that time, restoring what I lost during that period of separation.

I'm here to tell you that if he did it for me, he will do it for you. God says (see Isaiah 55:10–11) his Word will not return to him void, so put God to the test, and watch him prove himself to you.

Prayer Moment

Father God, in the name of your Son, Jesus Christ, I ask you to turn back the hand of time in my life and restore the things I lost, create new opportunities, restore strained relationship in my life. You said in your Word that you would repay the years the locust has eaten, and you turned back time for your servant Hezekiah. You are no respecter of persons, and if you did it for him, I know that you will do the same for me. I thank you right now in Jesus's name. Amen.

An Ambassador of the Kingdom of God

An ambassador is a diplomatic agent of the highest rank accredited to a foreign government or sovereign as the resident representative of his or her own government or sovereign or appointed for a special and often temporary diplomatic assignment.[1]

What does this mean to you? Second Corinthians 5:20 states that you are an ambassador of Christ. You are a direct representative of God just like Jesus Christ operated here in this earth. You are an authorized messenger of God, and through the Holy Spirit he has made available for you all the power needed for this position.

Prior to writing this book I had the opportunity to work with the U.S. Department of State and served at the American embassy in Singapore. During my tour of duty I had the opportunity to view how the U.S. ambassador to Singapore operated. While that person was serving as the American ambassador, he was the direct representative of the President of the United States.

When the ambassador spoke, it was treated as if the President of the United States was speaking. While he was living in that foreign country, the United States government provided a great benefits package to care for the well-being of the ambassador and his family. The U.S. government provided a home, vehicle, and household staff. All the ambassador had to do was to take care of the business of the United States of America.

Once you realize who you are in Christ Jesus, you will begin to function in the same capacity as an ambassador. During Jesus's ministry he functioned just like this after receiving the Holy Spirit. As you study the Scriptures, you will notice he didn't worry about his basic everyday needs; he was only concerned about fulfilling the Father's business (Luke 2:49, KJV). Jesus was in this world but not of this world's way of operating, and this is how you are to operate also. You are in this world fulfilling your purpose to set the example and tell those not yet in the kingdom of God what your Father has done for you.

Once you begin conducting yourself as an ambassador of Christ Jesus in your home, your workplace, and your community, you will begin to reap the same benefits as an ambassador. God will provide for all your needs. Put God in first place by dedicating your life to take care of his business on this earth, he will then fulfill his commitment to take care of your business.

Pause & Reflect

A king's power and authority are represented by his throne. A king can pass judgment and make decrees without leaving his seat of authority. When a king has an enemy within his region, he doesn't leave his throne to go and confront the enemy. The king will command his soldiers to go out and bring the enemy before him. Once the enemy is standing before the king, he issues a sentence and then sends him away. While he's accomplishing all those things, he never leaves his seat.

How does this relate to your life?

During this Christian walk there are going to be times when you are being attacked in different areas in your life. When your enemies arise with an attack to destroy you, you can remain in your seat of authority and pass judgment utilizing the Word of God. Begin to speak the Word of God over the situation:

> *No weapon that is formed against thee shall prosper; and every tongue that shall rise against thee in judgment thou shalt condemn. This is the heritage of the servants of the LORD, and their righteousness is of me, saith the LORD. (Isaiah 54:17, KJV)*

Don't fall into the temptation of getting even. Remain steadfast, and allow the Holy Spirit to guide you. He will direct you and tell you exactly how to proceed in whatever situations arise in your life. You will overcome all the challenges you face in life when you place your trust in God.

Dear friends, do not be surprised at the painful trial you are suffering, as though something strange were happening to you. But rejoice that you participate in the sufferings of Christ, so that you may be overjoyed when his glory is revealed. If you are insulted because of the name of Christ, you are blessed, for the Spirit of glory and of God rests on you. If you suffer, it should not be as a murderer or thief or any other kind of criminal, or even as a meddler. However, if you suffer as a Christian, do not be ashamed, but praise God that you bear that name. (1 Peter 4:12–16)

REVIEW

- You have been given all the power and authority to reign as kings in life through Christ Jesus. You are no longer controlled by the sinful nature of your flesh but the Spirit of God that lives in you.

- God has the ability to restore lost opportunities and relationships and place you where he ordained you to be.

- You are a direct representative of God just like Jesus Christ operated here in this earth. Once you realize who you are in Christ Jesus, you will begin to function in the same capacity as an ambassador.

Chapter 9
Principles of Holy Living

Since, then, you have been raised with Christ, set your hearts on things above, where Christ is seated at the right hand of God. Set your minds on things above, not on earthly things. For you died, and your life is now hidden with Christ in God. When Christ, who is your life, appears, then you also will appear with him in glory.

Put to death, therefore, whatever belongs to your earthly nature: sexual immorality, impurity, lust, evil desires and greed, which is idolatry. Because of these, the wrath of God is coming. You used to walk in these ways, in the life you once lived. But now you must rid yourselves of all such things as these: anger, rage, malice, slander, and filthy language from your lips. Do not lie to each other, since you have taken off your old self with its practices and have put on the new self, which is being renewed in knowledge in the image of its Creator. (Colossians 3:1–10, NIV APP)

Once you have accepted Christ, you should set your heart on the things above which requires you to place God's priorities first in your daily life. You are no longer part of this world, and you must cast down those earthly desires because Christ now dwells in you. This can be a challenge for your flesh, but you must get your flesh under the control of the Holy Spirit.

We must strive every day to live up to this expectation. As Christians we should set our minds to look at life from God's perspective, which is found in his Word, and to seek what he desires for us. The more we regard the world around us as God does, the more we will live in harmony with him.

Criticizing Others

How often have you throughout your life found yourself casting judgment on others? How many times have you found yourself pointing out other people's short comings? I want you to reflect on these questions, because this is a great hindrance to winning the unsaved for the kingdom of God.

In Matthew, Jesus tells us to examine our own motives and conduct instead of spending our energies judging others. The traits that bother us in others are often the habits we dislike in ourselves. Our untamed habits and behavior patterns are the very ones that we attempt to change in other people.

Do not judge, or you too will be judged. For in the same way you judge others, you will be judged, and with the measure you use, it will be measured to you.

> *Why do you look at the speck of sawdust in your brother's eye and pay no attention to the plank in your own eye? How can you say to your brother, 'Let me take the speck out of your eye,' when all the time there is a plank in your own eye? You hypocrite, first take the plank out of your own eye, and then you will see clearly to remove the speck from your brother's eye. (Matthew 7:1–5)*

As Christians, we are to utilize the examples Jesus provided during his life here on earth. Jesus said that we must examine ourselves before we cast judgment by criticizing others. We all have shortcomings, and until we are able to overcome our faults, what right does anyone have to criticize someone else?

The assignment of all Christians is to win souls for the kingdom of God, and in order to successfully accomplish this we must show love in everything we do. It is impossible to introduce someone to the love of God if the first thing that comes out of your mouth is what you think that person is doing wrong.

As a new Christian, you'll begin to see things in your life that you must remove or leave behind in order to grow in your relationship with God. As you begin to know God by studying the Scriptures, he will begin showing you how to remove hindrances and strongholds from your life. So don't let someone's criticism cause you to turn away from your Christian walk.

I need you to understand that once you accept Jesus as your Lord and Savior, you must know for yourself that this act is completed. No one needs to validate that you are saved, but you must be sure. Your salvation is based on your faith and trust in God, and your new lifestyle will show others of this change.

When Eliab, David's oldest brother, heard him speaking with the men, he burned with anger at him and asked, "Why have you come down here? And with whom did you leave those few sheep in the desert? I know how conceited you are and how wicked your heart is, you came down only to watch the battle."

"Now what have I done?" said David. "Can't I even speak?" He then turned away to someone else and brought up the same matter, and the men answered him as before. What David said was overheard and reported to Saul, and Saul sent for him.

David said to Saul, "Let no one lose heart on account of this Philistine; your servant will go and fight him." (1 Samuel 17:28–32)

In these verses we see that David didn't let the criticism of his oldest brother affect his purpose. David knew who he was, and he didn't care what others thought about him. I'm here to tell you to stand firm, believe in yourself, and don't let anyone's criticism stop you from serving God or fulfilling your purpose.

Most people believe that being a Christian is obeying a bunch of rules. That is totally untrue. Being a Christian is a way of life, and although you may strive to live a perfect life, at times you may fall short. That's okay because God is faithful and just to forgive you. Don't get me wrong: that doesn't give you a free pass to do what you want to do. But it is a promise from God letting you know that if you repent and turn from your sins, he will forgive you.

Where Is the Love?

How many times have you thrown around the word *love* expressing your feelings toward someone? How many times have you fallen out of love with someone? How many times has someone told you that they love you, but then their feelings changed?

I'm here to tell you that those questions do not represent the meaning of love. Love is a choice, not an obligation! Love is unconditional! You choose to love someone, and they choose to love you. When you truly love someone, it endures even when they are doing wrong. You are always willing to forgive that person. When you truly love someone, you put their feelings before you put your own. This is how God our Father and Jesus our Lord and Savior love us.

Jesus said the two greatest commandments are to love the Lord your God with all your heart, soul, and mind and to love your neighbor as yourself. The mission statement God gave me for my ministry is "Spreading God's love through random acts of kindness." It is my belief that the only way we can truly take this world away from the devil is to do what Jesus told us to do: Love your neighbor as yourself.

I've heard numerous pastors in my lifetime utilize this statement: "If you lift God up, he will do the drawing." I propose this question: "What are you lifting up?" It is not enough to just stand in front of large crowds and tell them what the Word of God says—although this is very important. However, you must also instruct them to put it in action.

How can you call yourself a Christian if you can't love your neighbor? How can you say you love the Father and Jesus whom you have never seen, and you can't love the neighbor you see every day? I pray that you will dig deep inside your heart and start loving those around you as Christ loves you.

Pressing toward Your Goal

After accepting Jesus Christ as your Lord and Savior, you must seek God and ask him to reveal your assignment. From the day you were created you were given an assignment to complete while on this earth. I don't know about you, but I don't want to stand before God without completing my assignment. One thing I've learned in this Christian walk is that your assignment is never just about you; it is always bigger than you. Your life assignment will help other people.

I may not be able to tell you the individual purpose God created you to accomplish, but he has called all born-again believers to win souls and make disciples for the kingdom of God.

You see, the devil has been a deceiver since the creation of the world, and he knows your end result. He will send attacks in your life more than ever in an attempt to get you to lose heart and give up. His desire is to deter you from the goal God has for your life. Prior to surrendering your life over to the Lord, you may have thought everything was going your way, but now that you are saved, you are encountering all types of problems.

I need you to understand that the devil no longer has any power to take anything from you. However, he can deceive and trick you into giving up before you obtain it. You must know that he is a defeated foe, and I encourage you to stand firm and push through until you obtain your goal. Remember that the Greater One is living on the inside of you.

Not that I have already obtained all this, or have already been made perfect, but I press on to take hold of that for which Christ Jesus took hold of me. Brothers,

I do not consider myself yet to have taken hold of it. But one thing I do: Forgetting what is behind and straining toward what is ahead. I press on toward the goal to win the prize for which God has called me he heavenward in Christ Jesus.

All of us who are mature should take such a view of things. And if on some point you think differently, that too God will make clear to you. Only let us live up to what we have already attained. (Philippians 3:12–16)

In this passage (see verse 10) Paul was talking about his goal to know Christ, to become like Christ, and to be all that Christ purposed him to become. The goal Paul set out to accomplish required intense pressure and absorbed most of his time and energy. This is a great example showing us not to take our eyes off our goal. With the single-mindedness of an athlete in training, we must lay aside everything harmful and forsake anything that may distract us from being effective Christians. What is holding you back?

We have all done things of which we are ashamed of, and we live in the tension of what we have been and what we want to be. But because our hope is in Christ, we can let go of past guilt and look forward to what God will enable us to become. Don't dwell on your past. Instead, grow in the knowledge of God by concentrating on your relationship with him now. Realize that you are forgiven, and then move on to a life of faith and obedience. Look forward to a fuller and more meaningful life because of your hope in Christ Jesus.

Perception Is Your Reality

In the olden days, sailors feared to venture far into the distant ocean because they thought the earth was flat as a table. They thought that when they reached the edge of the earth, they would slip down and perish in the bottomless ocean. We now know that is not true.

My question to you is, was the perception of the sailors the actual truth of the situation? No! Did they act and behave as if their perceptions were correct? They sure did. Dr. Wayne Dyer once said, "Change the way you look at things, and the things you look at change."**1** You may have heard the statement about the glass which some see as half full and others as half empty. The way we perceive things will determine the amount of success we experience. Perception can work either for us or against us. Which way do you choose to have it work for you?

As a Christian your perception affects the way you view people as well as the situations you may encounter. I wanted to address this issue so that you are aware that although your perception may be your reality, that doesn't mean that it is the reality of other people or even that it's factual.

As a child you may have grown up in an urban environment or the suburbs. You may be African American, Caucasian, Hispanic, or Asian, with different values that have been taught to you from your own social group or culture. You can conduct a survey with people of the same gender and age but with different backgrounds and ask them the same questions, and you will get different answers. Why do you think that is possible?

The answer is that we all come from different environments in which we were raised. Many adults tend to adopt values and act like the people within their own social group. That doesn't make the way you view things incorrect. Often you think or behave a certain way because you have adopted certain values to survive in your particular social group.

I want you to remember this issue before you begin judging others. Instead of getting upset when others think and behave differently, why not ask them to explain their point of view?

I believe that in order for you to be an effective witness for the kingdom of God, many times you need to find common ground in order to reach your hearers.

The Power of Sowing and Reaping

Sowing and reaping is a principle in the kingdom of God that all Christians need to understand. God's Word tells us what will happen in our lives when we honor and willingly give to him.

Whoever sows sparingly will also reap sparingly, and whoever sows generously will also reap generously. Each man should give what he has decided in his heart to give, not reluctantly or under compulsion, for God loves a cheerful giver. And God is able to make all grace abound to you, so that in all things at all times, having all that you need, you will abound in every good work. (2 Corinthians 9:6–8)

Many people become hesitant when you begin to discuss giving money. Maybe that is because they are used to providing for themselves, and they worry about having enough money left over to meet their own needs. Paul assured the Corinthians that God was able to meet their needs in all things and at all times. When you have developed the relationship of trusting your Father, he will place in your heart what to give and the purpose or plan to support. You must seek him even in this.

You also need to know that when giving, your attitude is more important than the amount you give. You do not give out of obligation but because you truly want to honor God.

Jesus sat down opposite the place where the offerings were put and watched the crowd putting their money into the temple treasury. Many rich people threw in large amounts. But a poor widow came and put in two very small copper coins, worth only a fraction of a penny. Calling his disciples to him, Jesus said, "I tell you the truth, this poor widow has put more into the treasury than all the others. They all gave out of their wealth; but she, out of her poverty, put in everything— all she had to live on." (Mark 12:41–44)

This woman gave out of her little. But because she put her faith in God, she put in more. When you know that your Father loves you, cares for all your needs, and will not harm you, you would then freely honor him with what you have. This type of attitude pleases the Father.

I want you to know that you should not be embarrassed if you can only give a small gift when you begin to give. God is concerned about how we give from the resources we currently have. Please don't allow lack of faith keep you from giving freely and generously and receiving all that God has available for you.

Church Denomination

There are reported to be over 38,000 Christian denominations. You may be wondering, "How do I choose which denomination to join?" You may also be wondering how you may know that the denomination you choose is correct.

Most people choose a denomination based on their emotions, and feelings. However you must understand that you should only choose a denomination based on accurate doctrine.

It is my belief that a specific denomination is not the only determining factor when choosing a church. There are many different types of denominations to appeal to different types of individuals. Your decision to choose a church should not be emotionally based. You should be led by the Spirit of God, and you need to do some research. What is the mission, what is the vision, what do they believe?

Wherever you are led, be sure it is a Bible-based church that believes that Jesus is the Son of God who died, was buried, and was resurrected and is now at the right hand of the Father and that we receive our salvation through our faith in him.

Pause & Reflect

I was raised in a Pentecostal church. As I continued my walk with Christ and visited other church denominations, I came to realize that we all had the same foundation, but different denominations focused on different parts of Jesus's message. I have now embraced all biblically based churches of sound doctrine, no matter what their denomination claims to represent. However, different denominations can keep God's people divided, and the devil utilizes these differences to exploit us.

I desire to teach all types of people no matter what their background. What is important to me is that you learn how to apply God's Word in your daily life and learn how much God the Father and Jesus the Son of God love you. That is the assignment God gave me, and that is what I promised him I would teach. I will be addressing the different types of denominations in great detail in my upcoming book, *Tearing Down the Walls of Tradition*, so please keep a lookout in your local bookstores later this year.

REVIEW

- You should set your heart on the things above, meaning place God's priorities first in your daily life. Set your mind to look at life from God's perspective, which is found in his Word, and to seek what he desires for you.

- With the single-mindedness of an athlete in training, we must lay aside everything harmful and forsake anything that may distract us from being effective Christians.

- When choosing a denomination, you should seek God and be led by the Holy Spirit.

- A person's perception is their reality.

- Love is a choice, not an obligation; love is unconditional.

- Examine our own motives and conduct instead of focusing our time judging others.

Chapter 10
Conclusion

The primary objective of this project was to motivate you by revealing just how much God the Father loves you and desires a relationship with you. The Bible is filled with many examples of men and women of God who have surrendered their lives to God and by faith fulfilled their life purposes. Their lives proved that in the midst of their challenges God was faithful, and their rewards were great.

A reward does not always come in the form of money as some may think, but may be an opportunity, a needed experience, or an idea. I encourage you, do not take your temporary discomforts personally. Go through your boot camp training, and gain the necessary skills you will need to walk out your purpose in life.

Remember the story of Job. Job lost everything he held dear to himself including his health. God had so much confidence in Job that he permitted the enemy to come in and wreak havoc in Job's life. God knew Job would not turn from his faith and the relationship he had developed with him. In the end Job did not turn from God, and all that Job lost was restored even more abundantly.

Most important, we have the life of Jesus as our example, and we should take this into account in our daily lives. Jesus loves us so much that he gave up his life for all mankind. His life is and will continue to be a blueprint for developing your relationship with the Father and walking through your transformation as a child of God. Accepting Jesus as your Lord and Savior will give you access to eternal life; however, God wants us to accomplish so much more. Many Christians complete this first step in their transformation and go no further. I encourage you not to stop just at the salvation of your soul, but continue in becoming a beacon of light in this world.

Receive the Holy Spirit, for he will help you complete this Christian way of life. The Holy Spirit will guide you, comfort you, and empower you to complete your assignment. As a Christian you have now taken on the role of an ambassador for the kingdom of God. You are the direct representative of God the Father on this earth, and you are obligated to take care of the business of the kingdom of God wherever God places you.

You may be operating in this world, but you are no longer of this world, this world's way of thinking. You are a citizen of the kingdom of God. The Bible outlines how a kingdom citizen operates, and I encourage you to study the Bible and learn how to function in your authority.

In this Christian life you must remain steadfast and endure to the end. The apostle Paul clearly stated, ***"One thing I do: Forgetting what is behind and straining toward what is ahead, I press on toward the goal to win the prize for which***

God has called me heavenward in Christ Jesus" (Philippians 3:13–14).

Living the life of a Christian is not about following rules, but it is a lifestyle. You now have a foundation to build upon, and I encourage you to join a Bible-based church that will not only teach you the Word of God but show you how to apply it to your everyday life. I pray that this project has given you insight and the drive to build that relationship with God the Father which will allow you to fulfill your divine destiny.

Book Notes

Introduction
1. Merriam-Webster Online, "Relationship," http://www.merriam-webster.com/

Chapter 1: Rewards
1. Merriam-Webster Online, "Rewards," http://www.merriam-webster.com

Chapter 2: How Much the Father Loves You
1. Merriam-Webster Online, "Love," http://www.merriam-webster.com/

Chapter 4: Jesus the Perfect Example
1. Merriam-Webster Online, "Mediator," http://www.merriam-webster.com/
2. Wikipedia online encyclopedia, "Hematidrosis," http://en.wikipedia.org/wiki/Hematidrosis

Chapter 7: Who Am I?

1. Merriam-Webster Online, "Ambassador," http://www.merriam-
   webster.com/

Chapter 8: Perception Is Your Reality

1. Thinkexist.com, "If you change the way you look at things,
   the things you look at change" Dr. Wayne Dyer
   http://thinkexist.com

About the Author

Cornelius Johnson is a native of Detroit, Michigan. He holds degrees in computer science and Christian studies. Cornelius served twelve years on active duty with the United States Marine Corps, after which he was hired as a network engineer working with the federal government. During this period Cornelius had the opportunity to live in numerous countries such as Japan, Okinawa, Korea, Singapore, Malaysia, Thailand, Cambodia, Nigeria, and Mauritania.

While living in these countries he had the opportunity to meet many people from different cultures and spiritual beliefs. These experiences gave Cornelius a worldwide view and the ability to relate to different individuals, cultures, and situations.

Cornelius has been preaching the gospel for seven years. He was ordained and appointed to the office of pastor under Household of Faith Pillar Ground of Truth Incorporated. He is the founder of Faith Life Fellowship and serves as lead pastor out of Houston, Texas.

This is the first of a three-book series as he prepares for a nationwide campaign, teaching people to complete their transformation into the likeness of God. Cornelius currently resides in Houston with his wife and two daughters.

For speaking engagements you can contact him as follows:

Cornelius Johnson
P.O. Box 3950
Humble, TX 77347
corneliusministries@gmail.com